T0334015

Cambridge Elements ⬛

Elements in Philosophy and Logic
edited by
Bradley Armour-Garb
SUNY Albany
Frederick Kroon
The University of Auckland

FREE LOGIC

A Generalization

Greg Frost-Arnold
Hobart and William Smith Colleges

CAMBRIDGE
UNIVERSITY PRESS

Shaftesbury Road, Cambridge CB2 8EA, United Kingdom

One Liberty Plaza, 20th Floor, New York, NY 10006, USA

477 Williamstown Road, Port Melbourne, VIC 3207, Australia

314–321, 3rd Floor, Plot 3, Splendor Forum, Jasola District Centre,
New Delhi – 110025, India

103 Penang Road, #05–06/07, Visioncrest Commercial, Singapore 238467

Cambridge University Press is part of Cambridge University Press & Assessment,
a department of the University of Cambridge.

We share the University's mission to contribute to society through the pursuit of
education, learning and research at the highest international levels of excellence.

www.cambridge.org
Information on this title: www.cambridge.org/9781009517874

DOI: 10.1017/9781009122764

First published 2024

A catalogue record for this publication is available from the British Library.

ISBN 978-1-009-51787-4 Hardback
ISBN 978-1-009-11405-9 Paperback
ISSN 2516-418X (online)
ISSN 2516-4171 (print)

Cambridge University Press & Assessment has no responsibility for the persistence
or accuracy of URLs for external or third-party internet websites referred to in this
publication and does not guarantee that any content on such websites is, or will
remain, accurate or appropriate.

Free Logic

A Generalization

Elements in Philosophy and Logic

DOI: 10.1017/9781009122764
First published online: August 2024

Greg Frost-Arnold
Hobart and William Smith Colleges

Author for correspondence: Greg Frost-Arnold, gfrost-arnold@hws.edu

Abstract: Classical logic assumes that names are univocal: Every name refers to exactly one existing individual. This Principle of Univocality has two parts: an existence assumption and a uniqueness assumption. The existence assumption holds that every name refers to *at least* one individual, and the uniqueness assumption states that every name refers to *at most* one individual. Various systems of free logic which have been developed and studied since the 1960s relax the existence assumption, but retain the uniqueness assumption. The present work investigates violations of both halves of the Principle of Univocality. That is, whereas the free logics developed from the 1960s are called 'free' because they are free of existential assumptions, the current Element generalizes this idea, to study logics that are free of uniqueness assumptions. It explores several versions of free logic, comparing their advantages and disadvantages. Applications of free logic to other areas of philosophy are explored.

Keywords: free logic, confusion, ambiguity, existence, Meinongianism

ISBNs: 9781009517874 (HB), 9781009114059 (PB), 9781009122764 (OC)
ISSNs: 2516-418X (online), 2516-4171 (print)

Contents

1 Introduction

Imagine that you are sitting in an introductory university course on the Ancient Mediterranean world, and the teacher poses the following questions: Did Homer exist? Did Hippocrates? Did the cities of Troy and Atlantis? These seem like substantial questions, which require serious archaeological and textual research to answer responsibly. At any rate, your teacher treats them that way, presenting various pieces of empirical evidence that bear on these questions, and describing competing historical hypotheses concerning these topics.

Now imagine that your next class that day is Introduction to Logic. You have just begun the section on first-order logic, and the teacher informs the class that standard first-order logic contains names. These names, the teacher tells you, must satisfy the

Principle of Univocality (PU): Every name refers to exactly one existing individual (Carnap, 1956, p. 98).

This Principle can be thought of as the conjunction of two components, namely, an existence condition and a uniqueness condition.

(PU-Existence) Every name refers to *at least* one existing individual.
(PU-Uniqueness) Every name refers to *at most* one existing individual.

For many names in ordinary language, both of these conditions hold. There is exactly one country currently named 'Zambia,' and exactly one number named by the numeral '7.' For other names, the uniqueness condition does not immediately hold, because many names are ambiguous (e.g., many people currently alive on Earth have the name 'María Rodríguez'). However, in most cases where uniqueness fails like this, speakers can easily disambiguate any ambiguous names they see or hear. For example, 'Paris' can be used to refer to a small town in northeast Texas, or the largest metropolis in France. Therefore, without further disambiguation, the sentence 'Paris has over 200,000 inhabitants' is ambiguous, and as a result it seems indeterminate whether that sentence is true or false, since the town in Texas has fewer than 200,000 inhabitants while the city in France has more than that number. However, if we replace the single name 'Paris' in our language with two names, 'Paris, France' and 'Paris, Texas,' then the ambiguity disappears. Each of those two names refers uniquely, and if we substitute exactly one of them into the previously indeterminate sentence in place of 'Paris,' the resulting sentence becomes true on the first disambiguation, and false on the second disambiguation. Hearers can also disambiguate based on context clues: If a speaker is talking about seeing the Mona Lisa last

Figure 1 Eiffel Tower in Paris, Texas, US.
Source: Carol Highsmith, commons.wikimedia.org/w/index.php?curid=51241417.

summer, then most likely any uses of 'Paris' will refer to Paris, France. (The speaker's use of the phrase 'Eiffel Tower' instead of 'Mona Lisa' would not necessarily have the same effect: The town in Texas has also built a structure it has named 'Eiffel Tower'; see Figure 1.)

However, we sometimes use names that do not satisfy the Principle of Univocality, and (unlike 'Paris') cannot be straightforwardly amended or disambiguated by context to meet that Principle. For example, when your Ancient history lecturer tells you 'The Greeks worshipped Zeus' or 'Atlantis never existed,' the names 'Zeus' and 'Atlantis' do not refer to anything that exists in the actual world (assuming the Ancient Greek myths and legends are not literally true). That is, the names 'Zeus' and 'Atlantis' do not satisfy (PU-Existence). And your ancient history lecturer also informs you that, given the evidence currently available to us, there was most likely no single person named 'Homer' who created the *Iliad* and the *Odyssey*. Rather, an oral tradition involving several people shaped the two epic poems that have come down to us. And the situation with the name 'Hippocrates' is somewhat similar. The set of medical texts we currently have from the Ancient Mediterranean, which initially appear to be written by a single physician, were most likely composed by several different people writing under the name 'Hippocrates.' We know relatively little about these people as individuals, besides the fact that each wrote a text that has been traditionally attributed to Hippocrates. Thus, we lack the resources needed to disambiguate the names 'Homer' and 'Hippocrates' successfully in the way we are able to disambiguate 'Paris.' Therefore, since the names 'Homer,' 'Hippocrates,' and 'Atlantis' violate the Principle of Univocality, you cannot use the tools you learned in your Introduction to Logic course to reason using sentences containing those names or ones like them, or to evaluate other people's reasoning when they use such sentences.

The field of free logic, traditionally understood, is a family of logics covering inferences involving 'Zeus,' 'Atlantis,' and similar names. The name 'free logic' abbreviates the full description of this field, namely: 'Logic of languages whose terms are free of existence assumptions.' In other words, in a free logic, unlike classical logic, (PU-Existence) need not hold. A logic is typically called 'free' if it allows languages to have names that fail to refer to anything existent, such as 'Zeus' and 'Atlantis.' Such terms are often called 'empty names.' As we will see in Section 3.4.4, on one version of free logic, 'Zeus' and 'Atlantis' can satisfy a weakened version of the Principle of Univocality, obtained by dropping the word 'existing' from the original formulation: If we allow names to refer to *non-existent things*, then the name 'Zeus' can refer to exactly one of those non-existing things. In such free logics, 'Zeus exists' is nonetheless false, because the quantifiers only range over existing things, and the quantifier $\exists$ is still used to express existence.

From the point of view of proof rules, the distinguishing feature of logics that allow for empty names is that the following two classical rules do not hold:

(Classical $\forall$-Elimination) Everything is F, therefore b is F
(Classical $\exists$-Introduction) b is F, therefore something is F

where F is any predicate and b is any name. For example, suppose it is true that everything is located somewhere in space and time. It does not follow that Zeus is located somewhere in space and time. The proof rules of free logics, unlike those of classical logics, capture that fact. Or consider the following informal argument and its formal regimentation:

Everything exists	$\forall x \exists y (x = y)$
Thus, Atlantis exists	$\therefore \exists y (a = y)$ (by $\forall$-Elimination)

(where 'a' abbreviates 'Atlantis'). This is valid in classical logic (assuming 'Atlantis' is a name), but it seems to be a pretty clearly invalid argument, from an intuitive standpoint. And it is in fact invalid in free logics. The core idea of the proof rules in free logic is to weaken the above two proof rules, by requiring an additional premise to use each rule:

(Free ∀-Elimination) Everything is F, b exists; therefore b is F
(Free ∃-Introduction) b is F, b exists; therefore something is F

where as before F is any predicate and b is any name.[1]

Logics that allow for empty names have been heavily studied and developed since the 1960s. An excellent, freely available, detailed introduction to much of this work that can be found in Nolt (2010); another very valuable overview is Lambert (2001). Both of those pieces should be mostly understandable to someone who has had a single logic course covering quantificational logic with identity. More advanced treatments are available in Bencivenga (2002) and Lehmann (2002). Because all these works are excellent, this text will not attempt to re-do what these authors have already done so well. Any reader who wants to fully understand the field of free logic as it currently stands is strongly encouraged to consult these resources, and I draw upon them substantially in the present work. Furthermore, these works cover certain important topics which the present work omits.

However, far less work has been done thus far on logics that relax the other half of the Principle of Univocality, namely the assumption that every name refers to at most one individual. A distinguishing feature of this Element is that it also investigates the logic of languages that fail to satisfy the uniqueness condition on names and predicates.[2] Subsequent sections examine not only languages that fail to meet (PU-Existence), but also languages that fail to satisfy (PU-Uniqueness). In other words, the present work takes the initial impetus of standard free logics one step further: Whereas long-standing free logics are only free of existence assumptions, the present work also discusses logics free of uniqueness assumptions for names and predicates. We can call logics that relax both the existence and uniqueness assumptions 'Generalized free logics.' There are several important logical parallels between logics that drop the existence assumption and those that drop the uniqueness assumption, but they also diverge in important ways. A central aim of this Element is to articulate those similarities as well as those differences.

Who is this book for? I have tried to write this Element so that almost all of it could be followed by someone who has taken a semester-long university

---

[1] This assumes the language has names. Even in languages without names, the free versions of these two rules are different from their classical versions; see p. 62 for the statement of these rules in a language without names.

[2] David Ripley (2018) explores failures of uniqueness at the level of sentences. Some failures of uniqueness first appear at the level of sentences, such as syntactic ambiguity ('The Japanese history teacher is tall').

course in first-order logic, such as is found in Barker-Plummer, Barwise, and Etchemendy (2011, ch. 1–13, 18) or the freely available Magnus et al. (2021, I–VII). Models will be treated more abstractly here, but the core ideas are the same as in the cited texts. Like those textbooks, the proofs here are presented in Fitch-style natural deduction format, so prior familiarity with that way of presenting formal proofs will be helpful. Parts of Section 4.3 will likely be the most difficult to follow for people without further background in logic.

I have attempted to make this Element useful and comprehensible not just to readers who are interested in free logic for its own sake, but also for people interested in metaphysics, philosophy of language, and philosophy of science. The central ideas motivating free logic, both in its standard, narrower form and the broader version presented in this Element, are directly relevant to these subfields of philosophy. So even if logic itself is not your primary focus, I hope the following pages contain some useful material for your primary interests.

2 Why Free Logic?

This section presents reasons for studying and using (generalized) free logic. If you believe there is in fact exactly one correct logic, you can take this section as providing reasons in favor of generalized free logic holding that title (or at least, for the characteristic features of generalized free logic being included in whatever your final preferred logic is). However, this section need not be understood as arguing that some version of free logic is the one correct logic. For even if you deny that there is one correct or best logic, that is, you are a logical pluralist like Beall and Restall (2006), you must still decide which particular logics are worth investigating and using. For there are infinitely many logics that potentially could be studied, and our time is finite. So for a pluralist, this section can be understood as arguing that generalized free logics should be among the few logics, selected from the infinity of all logics, that people actually devote time to investigating.

2.1 Human Languages Have Names That Are Not Univocal

The most straightforward reason to develop free logics is that the Principle of Univocality fails sometimes, and we would like to understand what effects such failures have on logic. We want to be able to reason logically about sentences containing terms like 'Atlantis' and 'Homer.' Ordinary languages contain names that apparently refer to nothing at all, such as 'Pegasus,' 'Santa Claus,' and 'Atlantis.' Such non-referring names are not restricted to myths, legends, and literary fictions. For example, in 2020, the *New York Times* ran an article with the seemingly paradoxical title "The Anonymous Professor

Who Wasn't", with the subheading "A professor at Arizona State University does not exist" (Bromwich & Marcus, 2020).[3] On Twitter, an account with the pseudonymous username 'Alepo' claimed to be a professor at Arizona State University. But as the *New York Times* article showed, Alepo never existed. The account was created by another professor, at a different university. Another famous example, often used in discussions of free logics, is the name 'Vulcan.' Several years before Einstein's General Theory of Relativity was proposed, astronomers noticed that their observations of Mercury's orbit conflicted with the predictions of Newtonian gravitation theory. To explain this discrepancy, the astronomer Le Verrier postulated the existence of a planet between Mercury and the Sun. He named this hypothesized planet, which we now know does not actually exist, 'Vulcan.' In short, the existence assumption of the Principle of Univocality fails sometimes.

There are also names that violate the uniqueness assumption of the Principle of Univocality. Joseph Camp offers a concrete example, which I shall use throughout to help fix ideas (Camp, 2002). Camp asks us to imagine a person, Fred, who goes to the pet store and purchases an ant colony in a box. The owner of the pet store tells Fred that every ant colony comes with many small ants and one big ant. When Fred gets home, he says "I'll call the big ant in this colony 'Charley'." Let us further suppose that Fred has not yet actually seen any of the ants at the moment of baptism. Unbeknownst to Fred, there was a mistake at the ant-farm factory, and there are actually *two* large ants in this colony. Let us call them 'Ant A' and 'Ant B.' These are names in our language, not in Fred's. Unfortunately, Fred is not very attentive, and when he opens up the ant-farm box and dumps all the ants into the farm, he fails to notice that there are two large ants in his colony. Further suppose that Fred never observes the two large ants simultaneously, and and as a result his language lacks names for Ant A and Ant B. But his language does contain the name 'Charley,' which can arguably be thought of as referring to both Ant A and Ant B (see Figure 2). There are too many ants, and not enough names (in Fred's language) to go around. (Further assume that neither Ant A nor Ant B is the "dominant causal source" of Fred's uses of the word 'Charley' and its associated mental representations, that is, Fred has as many interactions with one ant as he does with the other. For if Fred only ever saw Ant A, it would be reasonable to say that when he says 'Charley' that word refers to Ant A only [Lawlor 2007, p. 162].) If we think of the name 'Charley' as referring to multiple things, then we can describe 'Charley' as being ambiguous between

---

[3] https://www.nytimes.com/2020/08/04/style/college-coronavirus-hoax.html

Fred's
language

Unconfused
language

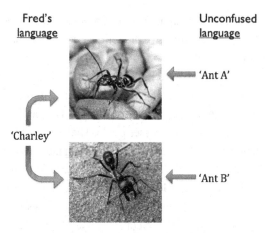

'Ant A'

'Charley'

'Ant B'

Figure 2 'Charley' visualized.
Source: Alexander Wild, www.alexanderwild.com/Professional/Public-Domain/.

Ant A and Ant B, or as conflating or confusing Ant A with Ant B.[4] But Fred does not explicitly think those thoughts – in this respect, he is even worse off than we are with respect to names like 'Homer' and 'Hippocrates,' since we at least know that those names do not refer to a single person. Graham Priest (1995, p. 369) offers another example of this type. Imagine an ameoba, which we name *a*. At some point after we named it, it undergoes binary fission, splitting into two nearly identical 'daughter' cells. According to Priest, the name *a* now multiply refers to both of the daughter cells.

Now, others may interpret the story of Fred (and Priest's ameoba) differently. Specifically, some may say that 'Charley' does not refer to both Ant A and Ant B, but rather refers to nothing at all: A singular term (such as a name) that does not pick out a single individual fails to refer to anything (Recanati, 2012). This way of thinking about 'Charley' is modeled logically by neutral and negative free logics (see Sections 3.2 and 3.3, respectively).

And there are real-life, modern-day examples of such ambiguous names, as well. For example, the figure at the center of the QAnon conspiracy theory, known only by the name 'Q,' is most likely two different people.[5]

---

[4] This is compatible with some of Fred's uses of 'Charley' referring to exactly one of the two ants. For example, if Fred is looking directly at Ant A, and says "Look! There's Charley!," that particular utterance of the word 'Charley,' on that occasion, plausibly refers to Ant A but not Ant B. Alternatively, we could say (following Kripke's terminology) that the "semantic reference" of 'Charley,' even in this situation, is still ambiguous between the two ants, but that the "speaker's reference" of that word on this occasion is Ant A only (Kripke, 1977).

[5] As a recent headline puts it, "QAnon's Mysterious Leader 'Q' Is Actually Multiple People" (Gilbert, 2020). This article is based on the research in an OrphAnalytics white paper (OrphAnalytics, 2020).

So such ambiguous names are not merely an artificial contrivance invented by philosophers or logicians to explore in the seminar room, but rather a naturally occurring linguistic phenomenon.

Failures of unique reference are not restricted to names. Definite descriptions, phrases of the form 'The F,' are another. Such phrases appear, from a linguistic point of view, to be singular terms, despite Bertrand Russell and his supporters' arguments to the contrary (see p. 17). That is to say: In felicitous circumstances, such phrases pick out exactly one existing individual. For example, 'The German Chancellor in 2015' picks out Angela Merkel. However, sometimes circumstances are not felicitous. Russell made famous the example of 'The current king of France.' This definite description does not refer to anything (that exists), even if you believe contra Russell that definite descriptions are singular terms. Definite descriptions can fail in the other direction too. For example, the phrase 'The US senator from New York in 2023' fails to refer uniquely to any individual, since there are two such senators (Chuck Schumer and Kirsten Gillibrand). Russell's way of handling problems arising from such cases of descriptions that fail to pick out a unique, existing individual denies that definite descriptions are singular terms; free logic allows for accounts of definite descriptions that make them singular terms, without requiring them to refer to exactly one existing individual.

Failures of uniqueness are not restricted to singular terms; predicates can be ambiguous too. For example, in chemistry, the simple term 'acid' has three definitions:

1. An *Arrhenius acid* increases the concentration of H^+ ions in water when dissolved.
2. A *Brønsted-Lowry* acid is a proton donor.
3. A *Lewis acid* can accept two electrons to make a covalent bond.

And in biology, the old term 'warm-blooded,' as applied to organisms, conflates three concepts scientists now consider distinct:

1. endothermic (primary energy source is food, not the sun)
2. tachymetabolic (faster metabolism)
3. homeothermic (roughly constant internal temperature)

Similarly, Sarah Richardson's (2022) work provides evidence that terms for biological sexes are potentially ambiguous: Are 'male' and 'female' about an organism's chromosomes, or quantities of estrogen (either currently or in the past), or quantities of testosterone? These variables can come apart. In some cases, scientists are clearly using a single one of these operationalizations of the terms 'male' or 'female.' But in other cases, they are not. In all three cases of 'acid,' 'warm-blooded,' and 'female,' many entities satisfy either all of the conditions, or none of them. So the ambiguity will often be inferentially harmless.[6] But the ambiguity is there, nonetheless.

2.2 Classical Logic Misclassifies the Logical Truths, or Restricts Logic's Applicability

One of the basic proof rules for classical first-order logic in a natural-deduction system is =-Introduction: For any name b, $b = b$. So, for example, if the phrase 'Angela Merkel' is a name, then 'Angela Merkel = Angela Merkel' is a theorem, and thus because first-order logic is sound,[7] it is a logical truth. A second basic proof-rule of classical first-order logic is ∃-Introduction: From $F(b)$, one can infer $\exists x F(x)$. So for example, given 'Angela Merkel was Chancellor of Germany in 2020,' the ∃-Introduction rule lets us derive 'Someone (or something) was Chancellor of Germany in 2020.' This particular example inference seems intuitively unobjectionable: If Merkel was chancellor, then it seems legitimate to infer that somebody or other was chancellor. However, when we combine these two rules, applying ∃-Introduction to 'Angela Merkel = Angela Merkel,' we can derive the sentence '$\exists x(x = $ Angela Merkel)$.$' This sentence is more colloquially paraphrased as 'Angela Merkel exists.' Now, simply from an intuitive point of view, many people feel that this sentence, though true, is not a *logical* truth. The fact that Angela Merkel exists does not intuitively seem like a matter of pure logic alone. Similarly, for any name b, the sentence $\exists x(x \neq b)$ is logically false in classical logic. But saying that this or that individual thing does not exist does not strike most people as *logically* false, even when it is false. To frame this point in terms of Ancient Greek philosophy: Standard textbook first-order logic in effect accepts Parmenides' claim that it is impossible to talk or think about individuals that do not exist (Priest, 2009, p. 236). The free logician, in contrast, attempts to formulate a logic in which Parmenides' view is not taken for granted in the logic itself.

Now, the classical logician could object to this reasoning as follows. Note that, at the beginning of the previous paragraph, we assumed that 'Angela

---

[6] Thus these are examples of what Stephen Yablo (2006) calls "non-catastrophic presupposition failure," the failed presupposition here being that the predicates 'acid,' 'warm-blooded,' and 'female' have unique extensions.

[7] Recall that a proof system is called *strongly sound* if every proof in that system is a truth-preserving argument in the chosen semantics. A proof system is *weakly sound* if every theorem (i.e., the last line of a proof with no premises) is a logical truth. Completeness is the converse. If a proof system is strongly complete, every truth-preserving argument has a proof using the proof-rules of the system. A proof system is weakly complete if and only if (henceforth, 'iff') every logical truth is a theorem. For each of soundness and completeness, the strong version entails the weak version, but not conversely.

Merkel' is a name. Our logic textbooks state that what it is to be a name in classical logic, from a semantic point of view, is just to be a term that refers to exactly one individual in the domain of quantification. If the semantic rules governing terms in the logic guarantee that a term t refers to exactly one individual in the domain, then $\exists x(x = t)$ is guaranteed to be true – and thus should be counted as a logical truth, contra the argument in the preceding paragraph.

This reasoning is impeccable: If b is guaranteed to refer to exactly one individual, then $\exists x(x = b)$ is guaranteed to be true. However, classical logicians still face an unpalatable dilemma, when they return to the sentence 'Angela Merkel exists.' Should it be considered a logical truth, or not? If the classical logician says it is *not* a logical truth, then 'Angela Merkel' must not be a name (in the logical sense described in the immediately preceding paragraph). But if you accept that, then you cannot apply the logical rules involving logical names ($\forall$-elimination and $\exists$-introduction) to ordinary-language sentences and inferences involving what we typically think of as names in ordinary language, like 'Angela Merkel.' Logic becomes inapplicable to our everyday reasoning about particular individuals, on this horn of the dilemma.[8]

If the defender of classical logic takes the other horn of the dilemma, then they can say 'Angela Merkel exists' *is* a logical truth, on the grounds that this English sentence should be formalized as $\exists x(x = b)$, where 'Angela Merkel' is symbolized as a name. But as was said three paragraphs ago, this sentence does not intuitively seem like a logical truth. And this intuitive feeling can be justified by appealing to certain conditions commonly placed on logical truth. Specifically, many people would like to accept the following three principles. All logical truths are (1) necessarily true (if anything is), (2) knowable a priori (if anything is), and (3) formal. But, as the next three subsections argue, '$\exists x(x = $ Angela Merkel$)$' is contingently true, only knowable a posteriori, and (at least arguably) not true solely in virtue of its grammatical or syntactic form. Summarizing the dilemma, the classical logician faces two unacceptable alternatives: Either 'Angela Merkel exists' is a logical truth, or the logical rules involving names ($\forall$-elimination and $\exists$-introduction) are not applicable to actual claims and arguments in ordinary language and thought. Free logic avoids both horns, by allowing names that do not refer to exactly one individual in the domain of quantification, and changing the proof rules accordingly.

---

[8] The end of Section 2.2.3 also argues that classical logic risks making logic inapplicable, but the argument below proceeds from a syntactic perspective, instead of the semantic point of view used here.

2.2.1 Logical Truths Are Necessary

First, Chancellor Merkel's existence is contingent. If her parents had never met, then she would never have existed. And it is possible that her parents might have never met: For example, one or both of them could have died in childhood. No contingent truths should be logical truths, yet the classical rules for =-Introduction and ∃-Introduction appear to make them just that, for classical logicians who think 'Angela Merkel' can be logically modeled as a name.

It is worth mentioning here a further subspecies of free logic, so-called universally free logic. Standard free logic, as we have seen, allows for names that have no referents. However, the semantics that is often presented for free logic requires, as a matter of logic, that at least one thing exists (in the technical language we will see in Section 3.1, the domain of quantification is not empty). And while it is incontrovertible that *something* actually exists (otherwise, with a nod to Descartes' *cogito*, who or what would be doing the controverting?), it is not obvious that it is logically necessary that something exists. In some nontrivial sense of 'could,' there could have been no individual entities. At least, it does not seem that logic alone requires that there be something rather than nothing. An 'inclusive' logic, unlike classical logic, is any logic that allows as a logical possibility the circumstance in which nothing exists. For example, consider the English sentence 'There is something that is either funny or not funny.' In classical first-order logic, this would be formalized as $\exists x(F(x) \vee \neg F(x))$. And this is provable in classical first-order logic. But in inclusive logics, it is not. A logic that is both inclusive and free is called 'universally free.' In sum, universally free logics, unlike classical logics, avoid committing to the view that it is necessary that there is something rather than nothing, and that Angela Merkel exists necessarily.[9]

2.2.2 Logical Truths Are Knowable a Priori

Second, we cannot know a priori that Angela Merkel exists. Most philosophers would agree that if a sentence expresses a logical truth, then that sentence can be known to be true a priori (if anything can – some philosophers claim that there

---

[9] Timothy Williamson (2002, 2013) argues that 'Angela Merkel exists necessarily' is true. Williamson's argument has faced substantial criticism, e.g., Rumfitt (2003). Another critic, Joshua Spencer (2013), claims that the truth of Williamson's conclusion is less plausible than the falsity of at least one of his premises, so Williamson's *modus ponens* should be re-cast as a *modus tollens*. And Spencer argues that the premise that is most likely to be false is 'Every declarative sentence is true or false.' As we will see in Sections 3.2 and 3.4.2, this rejection is independently motivated by leading proposals for the semantics of terms that violate the Principle of Univocality (as well as for other semantically 'defective' sentences, such as sentences that presuppose something incorrect).

is no a priori knowledge), provided one understands the language in which the sentence is written. But classical logicians cannot accept this principle, without denying that 'Angela Merkel' can be modeled logically as a name, thereby preventing us from applying the logical rules involving names to sentences containing 'Angela Merkel.' Whether Angela Merkel (or Zeus, or Homer) exists or not is an empirical, a posteriori matter. So the classical logician who treats 'Angela Merkel' as a name must deny the principle that all logical truths are a priori, on pain of holding that one can know a priori that Merkel exists and Zeus does not.

Free logicians, in contrast, can hold that 'Angela Merkel' is a name, and that logical truths are necessary and a priori. (We will turn to formality next.) One group ('positive' free logicians) make every instance of $s = s$, including 'Zeus = Zeus,' a logical truth (again, where s has all the grammatical features of a name). The rest ('negative' and 'neutral' free logicians) agree with the classical logician that 'Zeus = Zeus' is not a logical truth, but they do this by maintaining that *no* instances of $s = s$ are logical truths (though the neutral camp will say that $s = s$ is never false, as a matter of logic).

2.2.3 Logical Truths Are Formal

In any classical first-order logic, because of the Principle of Univocality, the string of characters 'Zeus = Zeus' is *not* a sentence (at least if 'Zeus' has its usual meaning of a non-existent Ancient Greek divinity, as opposed to naming my pet dog, for example). For in classical logic, the string of four letters 'Zeus' is not a genuine name, because (according to PU-Existence) every name refers to something existent, and Zeus does not exist. And since the only things allowed to appear on either side of the identity sign '=' are singular terms or variables (and 'Zeus' is definitely not a variable), 'Zeus = Zeus' is not a sentence in classical first-order logic. And so neither is '$\neg \exists x(x = \text{Zeus})$.'

This points toward a further problem for the classical logician. Namely, classical logic appears to be inconsistent with the claim that logical truth and theoremhood are always purely formal. Suppose s is a string of characters with all the grammatical or syntactic markers of a name of an individual; for example, combining s with any one-place predicate generates a grammatical sentence, but concatenating it with another name will not generate a grammatical sentence. (E.g., 'Kelly is tall' is a sentence, but 'Kelly Kelly' is not.) However, we leave it open whether s refers to exactly one individual, that is, we leave it open whether s meets the Principle of Univocality. As we just saw in the immediately preceding paragraph, the classical logician holds that some strings of characters with the form $s = s$ are *not* true (e.g., 'Zeus = Zeus'), while others are (when s is any symbol that the classical logician recognizes as a logical name). But this fact about classical logic conflicts with the widely accepted principle that a logical truth is true in virtue of its logical form (Gómez-Torrente, 2019). For example, Ludwig Wittgenstein wrote in a 1913 letter to Russell that "the propositions of logic – and only they – have the property that their truth or falsity, as the case may be, finds its expression in the very sign for the proposition" (von Wright, 1974, p. 42). In other words: If a string of characters is a logical truth, then every string with the same grammatical or syntactic form as that string is also true.

Using the completeness theorem, and substituting 'theorem' for 'logical truth,' we can derive an even more plausible principle than Wittgenstein's.[10]

(Theoremhood-Sentence Form) If a string of characters is a theorem, then every string that has the same grammatical or syntactic form as that string is also a theorem.

Now we can formulate the apparent dilemma for the classical logician. Let b be any symbol that the classical logician considers a name. '$b = b$' has the same grammatical or syntactic form as 'Zeus = Zeus': an apparent name, followed by the identity sign, followed by the same apparent name a second time. The classical logician now appears to be committed to the following inconsistent set of claims:

1. '$b = b$' is a theorem
2. 'Zeus = Zeus' is *not* a theorem
3. '$b = b$' has the same syntactic form as 'Zeus = Zeus'
4. the (Theoremhood-Sentence Form) principle above

If one prefers, this dilemma could be re-framed so that every instance of the word 'theorem' is replaced by 'logical truth,' and the Theoremhood-Sentence Form principle is replaced by Wittgenstein's principle. Bencivenga (2002, p. 173) makes essentially this argument, more concisely: "A logical truth should only depend on its (logical) form, and there seems to be no plausible (non *ad hoc*) ground for distinguishing between the form of 'Pegasus is white' and that of 'Secretariat is white'."

The classical logician can and should counter that point 3 above is false, since 'Zeus' does *not* have all the necessary syntactic features of a logical name in classical logic. For from a formal point of view, in order for a string of characters to be a classical name, that string must obey the classical proof rules involving names, namely ∀-Elimination ('Everything is F, therefore b is F,' for any name b and predicate F) and ∃-Introduction ('b is F, therefore something

---

[10] It is more plausible, because logical *truth* is still a semantic notion, whereas theoremhood and form are both fully syntactic.

[exists that] is *F*'). If a string of characters fails to obey all instances of those two rules, then that string is not a classical name, from the point of view of proof rules. And all sides of this debate agree that 'Zeus' does not obey these classical rules. For example, suppose that everything that exists must exist somewhere in space and time. But Zeus does not exist anywhere in space and time. So allowing the string 'Zeus' into the language as a name would generate instances of the classical ∀-Elimination rule that are invalid. And therefore, this classical logician concludes, 'Zeus' does *not* have all the grammatical characteristics of a name, and thus 'Zeus = Zeus' does not have the same syntactical form as 'Angela Merkel = Angela Merkel.' Therefore, the inconsistency described in claims 1–4 above disappears.[11]

Everything this classical logician says is correct. However, while this response does save the classical logician from inconsistency, it risks making classical logic nearly unusable as a tool for inferring new claims from old ones, that is, logic could not be used in the way it is typically used. For in order to make correct inferences using the classical rules of ∀-Elimination and ∃-Introduction, we must know whether an apparent name *s* is a genuine name (like 'Angela Merkel') or not (like 'Zeus' or 'Hippocrates'). But if the response of the preceding paragraph is correct, then we cannot know if *s* is a genuine name or not, unless we already know that every instance of ∀-Elimination and ∃-Introduction involving *s* is correct. Yet in general we want to use logic as a tool to reason (non-experientially) from previously known claims to uncover previously unknown (to us) claims. For example, a scientist uses logic to infer a prediction from a hypothesis. That is, we want to be able to *apply* ∀-Elimination and ∃-Introduction to existing information to infer new (to us) information. This would be impossible, if we have to know antecedently that every instance of those two proof rules involving a particular apparent name is correct. Free logic, in contrast, makes knowing whether a particular string *s* counts as a name much easier: You do not have to know that *s* refers to exactly one individual, or that it validates every instance of ∀-Elimination and ∃-Intro, in order to know that *s* is a name.[12] The free logician can know that 'Angela Merkel' and 'Zeus' can both be modeled logically as names.

---

[11] Thanks to Daniel Lindquist for discussion of the points of this paragraph.

[12] Lehmann (2002, p. 214) makes a similar point: "logical form," including whether an apparent name really is a genuine name, "should be reasonably accessible, and the closer it is to the surface form the better, other things equal. . . . If logical forms are contingent on whether certain expressions refer – a matter that may be very difficult to settle – then logic may not be very useful." Kroon (1991, p. 21) makes a stronger claim, with a similar conclusion: "[Q]uestions of logical syntax ought not to depend on purely contingent features of the world." This ties together the present point with Sections 2.2.1 and 2.2.2: Whether something is a name or not should be a matter of logical syntax, and logical syntax is not empirical or contingent.

In short, this section has argued that either classical first-order logic's characterization of the logical truths is too broad, or it makes logic inapplicable: It either counts certain truths, such as 'Indonesia exists,' as logical, which most people would say are not logical truths. Or if the classical logician instead claims 'Indonesia exists' is not a logical truth, then the applicability of logic to actual reasoning about particular individuals is threatened.

2.3 Philosophical Applications of Free Logic

Free logic can be of interest to logicians because of its distinctive logical properties, such as the failure of the rules of ∀-Elimination and ∃-Introduction in their classical formulations. However, philosophers who are not logicians can also find some use for free logic, since issues about non-existence and confusion appear independently in philosophy of language, metaphysics, and philosophy of science. This section briefly surveys some applications.

2.3.1 Philosophy of Language and Metaphysics

Negative existential claims, definite descriptions, empty names, and presentism. Philosophers have long been puzzled by statements about or involving non-existence. For example, the pre-Socratic Parmenides famously held that it is impossible to think about or talk about something that does not exist. For if you are literally thinking or talking of something that does not exist, then you are thinking of nothing; that is, you are not thinking about any thing at all. Classical Indian philosophers like Uddyotakara presented a very similar argument, in order to refute their Buddhist contemporaries who argued that the self does not exist (Chakrabarti, 1997, p. 211ff.). Roughly this same argument is studied nowadays under the title 'The problem of negative existential statements' (Clapp, Reimer, & Spire, 2019).

Put briefly, the problem is this. Consider the sentence 'Atlantis does not exist.' Most people (who are not conspiracy theorists) would say that sentence is true. But 'Atlantis' does not refer to anything that exists. However, one can now ask: *What* exactly is that true sentence talking about? Which entity is being discussed? If there is *no* entity being discussed, then it seems that our original sentence fails to convey the specific meaning we hoped to convey by uttering it. If we say that there *is* an entity being discussed, then it seems Atlantis does exist, and the sentence we initially thought was true has to be false instead. As we shall see in Section 3.4.4, Meinongianism is an attempt to block that inference: The Meinongian says that we can meaningfully and legitimately discuss an item or thing, without committing ourselves to that item *existing* in any sense. As Priest (2016, p. xxvii), who currently works in the Meinongian tradition, puts it: "Some things do not exist" (Priest, 2016, p. xxvii). People trained in the standard ways of regimenting English sentences into the symbolism of quantificational logic may hear that claim as a logical contradiction, despite it sounding like common sense to people who have not read logic textbooks. Priest, however, distinguishes between 'exists' and 'some.' He introduces a new quantifier for 'some' ($\mathfrak{S}$), and keeps the familiar existential quantifier with its usual meaning. He also introduces a predicate $E(x)$, which formalizes 'x exists.' So the English sentence 'Some things do not exist' is symbolized as $\mathfrak{S}x\neg E(x)$.

Many readers will know that one response to the problem of negative existentials, inaugurated by Bertrand Russell, is that there are not (or at least need not be, in scientifically respectable language) any genuine names, that is, terms that pick out individuals. Instead, words that have the surface appearance of names in our everyday language ('Angela Merkel,' 'Zeus') should instead be understood as having some other deep logical-grammatical nature. Russell thought what we typically consider names should be understood as definite descriptions ('the Chancellor of Germany from 2005 to 2021,' 'the divine being who lives atop Mount Olympus,' 'the author of the *Iliad*'), and that definite descriptions were not singular terms. That is, they should not be understood as referring to individuals. Instead, they are a special kind of quantifier (see three paragraphs below).

Quine suggested that we simply take apparent names as predicates: 'is Angela Merkel' would then be in the same logical category as 'is red' and 'is an apple.' Quine suggests introducing a predicate 'Angela-Merkelizes,' which is true of only Angela Merkel. This position, known as predicativism about names, is not the currently dominant view in philosophy of language, but in the last several years it has attracted some new defenders, after many years of unpopularity.[13]

This is an enormous issue, which is at the heart of central developments in twentieth century Anglophone philosophy, so there is not space to deal with it fully here.[14] If all apparent names are replaced by predicates or by definite descriptions that are not construed as singular terms, then there cannot be any violations of the Principle of Univocality for names, and thus the philosophical/logical problems about negative singular existence statements will disappear (since they become no more logically puzzling than 'There are no humans over

---

[13] See Sawyer (2020) for an overview of the arguments for predicativism about names, and Jeshion (2015) for arguments against it.

[14] See Bencivenga (2002, §§2-3) for an overview that pays particular attention to how this issue relates to free logics; Fitting & Mendelsohn, (1998, §8.4) also contains relevant logical discussion. For the early history of empty names more generally, see Textor (2016).

ten feet tall'). However, note that the uniqueness-free languages described in this Element allow non-univocal *predicates*, and thus also for non-univocal definite descriptions, such as 'the current US senator from California' (since each US state has two senators).

Furthermore, another motivation for pursuing free logics is the desire for alternatives to Russell's theory of definite descriptions. As is well known, this theory states that a sentence of the form 'The F is G' is true exactly when (i) there is at least one F, (ii) there is at most one F, and (iii) that one F is G. Formally, Russell's theory states (where '$\imath x F(x)$' symbolizes 'the F'):

$$G(\imath x F(x)) \;\leftrightarrow\; \exists x[F(x) \wedge \forall y(F(y) \rightarrow y = x) \wedge G(x)] \qquad \text{(RussellDD)}$$

One criticism of Russell's theory of definite descriptions is that from a linguistic point of view, 'The F' appears very much to be a singular term, that is, a term that picks out an individual, but Russell's theory does not treat it as such, contrary to the linguistic evidence. So one might want a theory of definite descriptions that can classify them as singular terms (Morscher & Simons, 2001, p. 20), (Lambert & van Fraassen, 1972, p. 152). Since the core idea of free logic is to allow singular terms that fail to refer to exactly one individual, free logic appears naturally positioned to provide an alternative to Russell's theory.

The problem of negative existentials is closely related to the more general 'Problem of Empty Names.' In general, the truth-value of a sentence is determined by the referents (extensions) of the phrases in it, plus the syntactic arrangement (i.e., logical form) of those phrases. So, in a grammatical sentence with a (purported, apparent) name, if that name does not refer, then there will be a 'blank' or missing semantic component in that sentence – a missing component that would prevent the sentence from having any truth-value. To take a simple example, the true sentence 'Quito is a capital' has the grammatical form: *name + copula + one-place predicate*. For this sentence to have a truth-value at all, it seems very plausible that the name must refer to something, since a string of words that is just a copula and a predicate (such as 'is a capital'), considered by itself, cannot express a (full, whole) proposition. The Problem of Empty Names is the set of difficulties involved in interpreting sentences that seem to have a semantic 'blank' where a (single) individual should be.

The Problem of Empty Names threatens to make communication between people who have different beliefs about what exists impossible: If failures of univocal reference make sentences unable to (be used to) communicate full, meaningful propositions, then ontological disagreements threaten to become linguistically impossible. As Greg Restall (2019, p. 11) puts it, "We would very much like to allow the use of logical techniques in a discussion where we have participants who disagree not only about what is the case, but also disagree about what there is – in a shared vocabulary with an agreed upon syntactic regimentation." One advantage of a free logic over classical logic is that free logics allow for such direct disagreements in a common language.

For example, consider the debate in philosophy of time between presentists and eternalists: Do only present things exist, or do past and future things exist, as well as present things? The presentist says that, for example, Napoleon Bonaparte does not exist (though of course he once did); the eternalist allows that Napoleon does exist (for he is not a fictional or mythical character). Without using a free logic as the background logic in which to frame the debate, the presentist's claim 'Napoleon does not exist' either does not express a complete proposition (if the presentist says 'Napoleon' lacks a referent) or is logically false (if 'Napoleon' is treated as a legitimate name).[15] And even the critics of presentism do not think that this is the right kind of reason to reject presentism: The real debate lies elsewhere.[16]

Teleosemantics.   Uniqueness-free logics can be used to articulate more precisely philosophical debates that crucially involve conflation, confusion, and certain types of indeterminacy. For example, so-called teleosemantic theories of content are often thought to face indeterminacy problems (Neander, 2017, ch. 7). Teleosemantics attempts to provide a completely naturalistic theory of representation, that is, a scientifically respectable account of under what circumstances one thing represents (i.e., is about) another; the most commonly discussed case is how a particular mental state in a particular organism represents a particular state of affairs in the world rather than another. There are a wide variety of teleosemantic theories of content (Schulte & Neander, 2022, §3), but the core idea is that the content of a representation is determined (at least in large part) by its function. And functions are explained naturalistically, for example, by natural selection (the function of an organ is whatever it was selected for) or learning processes. Why do some people think this would lead to indeterminacy of content? A commonly used example here involves the fly-catching system of the frog. "The frog's visual system is designed so that a fast moving dark object flying through the visual field will trigger a certain response; it shoots out its tongue and attempts to capture the object" (Agar, 1993, p. 2). Many people find it very likely that there is some cognitive state in the frog that comes between the visual stimulus and the tongue snapping. But what, exactly, does that cognitive state represent

---

[15]   Assuming names such as 'Napoleon Bonaparte' are not predicates.

[16]   For more on free logic and presentism, see Sullivan (2012) for more on the logic, and Paoletti (2016) for a Meinongian treatment.

(if anything)? Indeterminacy appears here, because there seem to be multiple plausible candidate answers teleosemantics could give to this question. It could represent a fly (of a particular species? A particular genus?), or frog-food, or a small, fast-moving, dark object. Each of these would play a role in increasing the frog's fitness in typical frog environments ('typical' is necessary, since in an environment with many small, fast-moving, dark objects that are poisonous to frogs, such a representation triggering a tongue-flick would not be adaptive). Different versions of teleosemantics are distinguished, in part, by adding further conditions that pick out just one of the candidates. There is a massive amount of debate about which of these various proposals is best. But perhaps, as Karl Bergman (2023) suggests, we should stop trying to figure out which one of these candidate contents is correct, and instead simply think of the content of the frog's representation as genuinely indeterminate between the candidate contents. We could use a uniqueness-free language to say, in a logically regimented way, that the frog's cognitive state signifies all three (and others besides). Some philosophers may fear that representational indeterminacy threatens some sort of conceptual incoherence or other cognitive disaster. But if we have a logic that allows for limited indeterminacy as a matter of course, then Bergman's proposal to embrace the apparent representational indeterminacy of teleosemantics can be considered as a genuine, conceptually coherent alternative.

Transparency of mental content and slow-switch cases.   Another area in philosophy of language and mind in which uniqueness-free logic could be relevant is semantic externalism, and in particular, debates about so-called slow-switch cases. To understand slow-switch cases (and semantic externalism), we need the concept of Twin Earth. Twin Earth is a place where things have the same easily observable properties as things on our Earth do, but are chemically very different. So for example, on Twin Earth, there is a shiny yellow ductile metal that is often fashioned into jewelry and used for exchanging wedding vows. However, this stuff, at the atomic level, is not what we call 'gold,' that is, an element with seventy-nine protons. Instead, this stuff on Twin Earth has a different chemical formula, which we will abbreviate ABC. Confusingly for us on Earth, the word for ABC on Twin Earth is also 'gold.' But (at least according to the semantic externalist) the word 'gold' has a different meaning for the inhabitants of Twin Earth than it does for us here on Earth, and thoughts involving the concept GOLD are different for inhabitants of the two planets.

The following is an example of what Tyler Burge (1988) calls a 'slow-switch' case. Imagine a person just like you who is born on (regular) Earth, lives there for several years, and is exposed to a normal amount of gold, and a normal amount of people talking about gold. Then, one night, interstellar visitors from Twin Earth abduct this person in their sleep, taking them to Twin Earth. But when the traveler wakes up, it appears to them that they are in their usual bed, surrounded by the usual people, in their usual neighborhood. In other words, from their point of view, there have been no detectable changes. This is called a 'slow-switch' case, because it seems that the contents of our traveler's words and thoughts slowly switch from their Earth-contents to the new Twin-Earth-contents. For example, when the traveler wakes up on their first day on Twin Earth, before they have interacted with any ABC, or talked to anyone on Twin Earth, they may wonder 'Is my favorite gold necklace in the drawer?' Many people have the intuition that 'gold' here is still referring to the element with seventy-nine protons, not ABC. But after our traveler has lived on Twin Earth for twenty years, then their utterances of 'gold' will refer to ABC instead.

Now imagine our traveler, after first living on Earth for twenty years, and then living on Twin Earth for twenty years, engages in the following simple reasoning:

(P1) When I was a child, my mother's favorite necklace was made of gold.
(P2) My current favorite ring is made of gold.
    Thus, my current favorite ring, and my mother's favorite necklace when I was a child, are both made of gold.

How should we understand this reasoning? If we accept the intuitions described in the immediately preceding paragraph, then both premises are true, but the conclusion cannot be true. Thus, the traveler commits a fallacy of equivocation: 'gold' means Earth-gold in P1, but means Twin-gold in P2. Fallacies of equivocation of course happen in everyday life. But in the slow-switch case, unlike everyday cases, the traveler is "in principle not in a position to notice" this equivocation (Boghossian, 1992, p. 22). And if this is correct, then according to Boghossian, logical reasoning is no longer a priori: Whether a particular inference is valid or invalid (because equivocal) depends on whether or not the reasoner has been kidnapped and taken to Twin Earth without their knowledge.

Furthermore, a principle called 'Epistemic Transparency' about your own concepts seems to be violated by the slow-switch case. This principle states: "[P]rovided that you are minimally rational, you simply cannot mistake one conceptual content for another" (Schroeter, 2007, p. 597). Here is an alternative formulation, also drawing on Schroeter: "If it seems to you that two tokens [e.g. 'gold' in P1 and 'gold' in P2] 'obviously and uncontrovertibly' mean the same, then they do mean the same and [because meaning determines reference] co-refer (if they refer at all)" (Recanati, 2012, p. 117–118). And from the traveler's point of view, the concept GOLD occurring in the P1-thought is no different from the concept GOLD occurring in the P2-thought; they "seem to" the traveler to "obviously and incontrovertably mean the same" – if anything does. And if epistemic transparency fails, then you cannot tell if $F(a)$ and $F(a)$ are the same belief or different beliefs. And if you can't determine that, then you cannot tell whether two claims contradict each other: $\neg F(a)$ might not contradict $F(a)$, since you do not know if those two 'a's have the same meaning, or if those two 'F's have the same meaning.

People have proposed various ways to avoid drawing this unwelcome conclusion from the slow-switch cases. Recanati offers one: He proposes that 'gold' in the above argument fails to refer in both P1 and P2. On his view, the traveler "is confused: he uses a single mental file [roughly, a concept of an individual] to refer to two distinct objects. This can only generate reference failure: the file the subject deploys in thought does not refer" (Recanati, 2012, p. 142). As a result, both premises are neither true nor false (Recanati, 2012, p. 131). Thus the validity of the argument is saved, so logic can still be a priori. This also allows Recanati to save epistemic transparency, by relying on a proviso in the statement of the principle. Recall one version of the principle: "If it seems to you that two tokens 'obviously and uncontrovertibly' mean the same, then they do mean the same and co-refer (*if they refer at all*)" (Recanati, 2012, p. 117–118). Since Recanati holds that both appearances of 'gold' in the slow-switch argument do not refer to anything, they are not counter-examples to epistemic transparency on his view, since the italicized condition is not met.

It is clear that Recanati assumes arguments involving confused words and concepts follow a neutral semantics for free logic (Section 3.2). He does not entertain the alternative options that P1 and P2 should be understood as false (as negative free logic would have it), or that 'gold' in all three lines of the argument could refer both to the element with seventy-nine protons, and to the stuff with molecular composition ABC. By itself, this is of course not an objection to Recanati's position. But it does open up further lines of inquiry about slow-switch cases. Since Recanati is (implicitly) using a neutral semantics, his view will have all the advantages and disadvantages of neutral semantics more generally (Section 5.1). Situating his position within the discussion about the pros and cons of various semantics for free logics immediately delivers a fuller evaluation of his position on slow-switch cases in particular, and confusion more generally. Additionally, if someone is broadly sympathetic to Recanati's overall position, but finds some of the particulars unpalatable (is the traveler really failing to have any thought whatsoever?), then alternative understandings of confusion are available, which may avoid some of the more undesirable consequences of Recanati's specific proposal.

Free logic should not be expected, on its own, to solve the presentism versus actualism debate, the problem of negative existentials, how best to formulate a teleosemantic theory of content, or how to understand slow-switch cases. But free logic can nonetheless be of use in these debates. It can help with precise formulations of various positions one might take in this debate, and perhaps more importantly with tracing out the logical consequences of the various positions. In particular, a position that might seem fairly plausible when initially characterized in everyday language might nonetheless logically entail some highly unintuitive consequences, which only become apparent after the position is stated rigorously. Put otherwise, free logic can help make explicit the various positions in the debates over empty or ambiguous names, thereby also making clear each position's costs and benefits. And it can also provide a framework that does not make opposing sides in disagreements over what exists incomprehensible to each other.

2.3.2 Philosophy of Science

The problems of defective reference mentioned in Section 2.3.1 feed directly into issues in philosophy of science. That may sound surprising to some, since philosophy of science is not integrated very closely with work in the philosophy of language, especially compared to the middle twentieth century. I will briefly discuss two applications of free logic in philosophy of science: how to understand the moral of the so-called Pessimistic Induction over the history of science, and the nature and implications of Thomas Kuhn's notion of incommensurability.

The Pessimistic Induction.　The Pessimistic Induction over the history of science is an argument against the view that current scientific theories are probably approximately true. Scientific realists typically argue that current scientific theories are approximately true, on the grounds that these theories make predictions about observable things that turn out to be incredibly accurate. However, a critic of this argument could point out that, for example, Newtonian mechanics and gravitation were (considered) extremely well confirmed in 1800, because they made extremely accurate predictions about a variety of observable events. Nonetheless, Newton's theories have since been supplanted by quantum mechanics and general relativity, and the fundamental picture of the physical world provided by those two theories is very different from that of Newton. The Pessimistic Induction is a generalization of this example: From the (purported) fact that most past scientific theories turned out to be incorrect in important ways, the pessimistic inductor concludes that our currently accepted theories will also turn out to be importantly untrue as well.

The Pessimistic Induction has been widely discussed; a short Element on free logic is not the place to delve into these debates. But which type of free logic one adopts – positive, negative, or neutral – will have important consequences for debates about the Pessimistic Induction. As explained briefly in the final paragraph of Section 2.3.2, positive, negative, and neutral free logics are distinguished by how they view atomic sentences containing defective terms (like 'Vulcan' and 'Charley'): Negative free logics say they are all false, positive free logics say at least one is true, and neutral free logics say such atomic sentences are neither true nor false. So, if one accepts neutral free logic or one of the positive free logics that allow some sentences to be neither true nor false, and is also committed to the anti-realist thesis that there are many non-referring and/or ambiguous terms in the language of superseded scientific theories (for example, 'phlogiston,'[17] 'caloric,'[18] or 'is simultaneous with'[19]), then one will believe that past theoretical claims containing such terms are not false, but rather truth-valueless.[20] Now, one might think this distinction is unimportant: Both ways count as being incorrect, neither is true. However, this difference matters, because the vast majority of current scientific anti-realists would characterize themselves as epistemic anti-realists, but semantic realists. That is, most anti-realists today wish to draw a contrast between their anti-realism and (versions of) instrumentalism of the early twentieth century. This instrumentalism maintains that scientific theories are merely tools for prediction and control, tools which are not the kinds of things that can be true or false: A hammer is neither true nor false, but rather more or less useful for a particular task. That is, these earlier instrumentalists were semantic anti-realists. But at least since van Fraassen (1980), the dominant anti-realist view has been that theoretical claims are either true or false (semantic realism), but that the evidence available to us does not justify our believing those theories to be even approximately true (epistemic anti-realism).[21] Many people, several

---

[17] Phlogiston was hypothesized to explain, among other things, why some substances burned and others did not. Highly combustible substances were believed to be rich in caloric; combustion released phlogiston from the substance. This explains why a log is heavier than the ash it becomes after burning: It has lost its phlogiston.

[18] Caloric was posited to be the material fluid of heat. Hasok Chang (2003) argues that the case of caloric is good evidence in favor of anti-realism.

[19] In special relativity, as opposed to classical mechanics, whether two events are simultaneous is relative to an inertial frame of reference.

[20] Darrell Rowbottom (2022) argues that some strictly truth-valueless sentences can nonetheless be approximately true. Since the scientific realism debate is about approximate truth instead of strict truth, a realist could accept that certain scientific sentences are, strictly speaking, truth-valueless.

[21] However, Rowbottom (2011; 2019, Ch. 2) attempts to re-invigorate semantic anti-realism in philosophy of science.

anti-realists included, would reject a position that entails semantic anti-realism. As the saying goes, one person's *modus tollens* is another's interesting *modus ponens*, so a committed anti-realist could view this as a way to construct an argument for semantic anti-realism.

So free logic bears on the scientific realism debates: Which version of free logic one adopts (positive, negative, or neutral) affects whether you are a semantic realist or not (Frost-Arnold, 2014). Finally, it should be noted that this is not only an issue for anti-realists; scientific realists also need to have some semantic account of apparently defective terms like 'caloric' and 'phlogiston.' Free logics, and in particular positive free logics, could be used to defend a realist position, since positive free logics allow speakers to state truths even when the language they are using harbors incorrect presuppositions (from their successors' point of view).

Semantic incommensurability.   One of Thomas Kuhn's characteristic ideas is the claim that, after a scientific revolution occurs, the pre-revolutionary theory and post-revolutionary theory are incommensurable. Kuhn discusses different types of incommensurabilities, including incommensurability of methodologies and incommensurability of weights of criteria for choosing a theory. (For example, if simplicity is very important to me but scope of application is not, whereas broad scope is important to you but simplicity is not, then you and I may have an irresolvable disagreement about which of two theories is better supported by our shared available evidence; see Kuhn [1977].) That said, the type of incommensurability that Kuhn increasingly stressed later in his career was semantic incommensurability (Sankey, 1993); Paul Feyerabend (1981) also famously argued for this type of incommensurability between earlier and later scientific theories. The core idea is that certain terms in the language of pre-revolutionary science cannot be expressed in the post-revolutionary language, or vice versa, and this entails that we cannot fully compare the two theories, that is, they are incommensurable. For example, there is simply no way to capture perfectly, within a relativistic conceptual framework, the Newtonian assertion that the Sun is at absolute rest, since neither the term 'absolute velocity,' nor sentences containing that term, can be translated into relativistic language without changing the meaning of the original, pre-relativistic assertion. In short, if a term (or sentence) cannot be translated without loss from the pre-revolutionary language into the post-revolutionary language, or conversely, then the two theories cannot be meaningfully compared (at least on those claims only expressible in the contested language: There might be other parts of the languages where an acceptable translation is possible). There is no shared, mutually comprehensible medium for expressing thoughts.

However, generalized free logic can arguably reduce some (though not all) of the incommensurability that results from untranslatability. That is, the fact that an assertion stated in pre-revolutionary vocabulary cannot be translated without loss into an equivalent assertion in the post-revolutionary language does not entail that the truth-value of a pre-revolutionary assertion cannot be assessed within post-revolutionary language. Hartry Field (1973) pioneered this idea, so we will use his central example. He noted that special relativity deploys two concepts of mass (relativistic mass, which is the total energy divided by the speed of light squared, and proper mass, which is the *non*-kinetic energy of a body divided by the speed of light squared), where pre-relativistic physics used just one. In other words, from a special-relativistic point of view, the single Newtonian word 'mass' conflates 'relativistic mass' and 'proper mass.' Thus, there is no way to translate claims involving the term 'mass' between the two languages. However, Field proposes a way, from within the special-relativistic language, to declare certain Newtonian sentences involving 'mass' to be true or false. When a Newtonian says 'The mass of the Earth is less than that of the Sun,' a relativist can declare that to be true, on the grounds that the relativistic mass and the proper mass of the Earth are both less than those of the Sun. And on Field's proposal, the sentence 'The mass of the Earth is greater than the mass of Jupiter' is false within the relativist framework, because both the relativistic mass and the proper mass of the Earth is less than the relativistic mass and proper mass of Jupiter. The only time, on Field's proposal, a relativist cannot assign a truth value to a Newtonian claim involving 'mass' is when the Newtonian sentence is true of proper mass and false of relativistic mass, or vice versa (for example, the Newtonian sentence 'A body's mass does not change when its velocity changes,' which is true of proper mass but false of relativistic mass). Generalizing from this case, Field's proposal is the following. For a sentence containing a confused or ambiguous term, that sentence is (i) true if and only if it is true on all disambiguations, (ii) false if and only if it is false on all disambiguations, and (iii) truth-valueless if that sentence is true on some disambiguations but not on others. This is called a 'supervaluational' semantics; if one does not want to identify 'truth on all disambiguations' with 'truth' itself, the former is labeled 'supertruth.' Supervaluational semantics like Field's are one kind of positive semantics for free logic. They will be discussed at greater length in Section 3.4.2.

In sum, generalized free logic is interesting from a logical point of view, and there are plausible reasons to study it for its own sake. Imposing the Principle of

Univocality is at odds with actual human languages, unnecessarily restricts the languages whose logical behavior we can study, and makes certain sentences into logical truths that, at least at first glance, do not appear to be logical truths. But there are also 'instrumental' or applied reasons to be interested in free logics as well: Significant questions in metaphysics, philosophy of language, and philosophy of science depend on how the details of one's free logic are developed. And certain ontological questions cannot even be coherently, intelligibly asked within classical logic.

3 Truth and Models

As mentioned in the previous section, there are multiple species of free logic. Every free logic is standardly classified as exactly one of positive, negative, or neutral. The semantic way of classifying these species of free logic is as follows. Let us define a 'defective' name as a string of characters that has the grammatical properties of a name, but violates the Principle of Univocality, such as 'Santa Claus' or 'Homer.' In positive free logics, there is at least one atomic sentence containing a defective name that is true (for example, 'Santa Claus = Santa Claus'). In negative free logics, every atomic sentence containing a defective name is false. And in neutral free logics, all atomic sentences containing a defective name are neither true nor false. This chapter presents model-theoretic semantics for each of these three types of free logic.

The above taxonomy has been completely standard for decades. Once we move to the 'generalized free logic' proposed in this book, a further taxonomy becomes available. When originally introduced in the 1960s, the name 'free logic' abbreviated the longer phrase 'logic free of existential assumptions.' But if one also wishes to eliminate uniqueness assumptions, then we can distinguish between three cases: (i) logics that relax the existence assumption, (ii) logics that relax the uniqueness assumption, and (iii) logics that relax both. Traditionally, the phrase 'free logic' refers to (i); here, we will call (i) 'existentially free logic.' We will use 'uniqueness-free logic' to refer to (ii); (ii) can also be thought of as the logic of ambiguity and/or confusion. Finally (iii) will be 'generalized free logic,' since it generalizes from only relaxing existence assumptions to also include relaxing uniqueness assumptions.

At the broadest level, this section follows the standard classification system of positive, negative, and neutral semantics. But within each of these species, I will note logical differences between languages whose only defective names refer to nothing, and those whose only defective names refer to more than one individual.

3.1 Shared Preliminaries

Generalized free logic results from making small modifications to (so-called) classical first-order logic. Thus, before we describe the various semantics for free logic, we must first set out terminology and notation for classical first-order semantics or model theory.

We begin with purely grammatical specification of a first-order language. This should be familiar from any logic textbook, but I spell it out here to fix notation. A language L contains:

- names of individuals: $a, b, c, \ldots$
- individual variables: $x, y, z, w, \ldots$
- predicates, each with a fixed number of one or more places: $F(x)$, $G(x,y)$, $H(x,y,z) \ldots$
- quantifiers: $\exists$ ('there exist(s)') and $\forall$ ('every,' 'all')
- sentential connectives: $\wedge$ ('and'), $\vee$ ('or'), $\neg$ ('not'), $\rightarrow$ ('only if')
- opening and closing parentheses: (,)
- *(optional)* the identity predicate '$=$'

The definition of the language L is given by a (typically recursive) definition of 'sentence' for strings of the above characters. That is, the definition of L effectively specifies which ordered combinations of the above characters count as (closed) sentences, and which combinations do not. So, for typical first-order languages, $G(a,b)$ is sentence, whereas $G(x,b)$ is not. And this matches ordinary English: 'Algeria is greater in size than Belgium' is a complete sentence, whereas 'x is greater in size than Belgium' is not.

The specification of L is purely grammatical or syntactic; that is, it does not depend at all on the meanings of the characters listed above. Meanings are introduced via a *model*. A classical model $M = \langle D, f \rangle$ of a language L consists of a non-empty domain or universe of individual elements D, and an interpretation function f. The interpretation function takes (combinations of) the linguistic items listed above as inputs, and assigns them set-theoretical entities as outputs. Specifically, the interpretation function assigns to each name of L an individual in D, and takes each n-place predicate of L to a set of ordered n-tuples in D^n. So for example, let D be the cities in the world with a population over 1,000,000 at any point in 2020. Also let $f(a) =$ Hong Kong, and $f(b) =$ Barcelona. Now suppose we introduce the two-place predicate $P(x,y)$ as a formal correlate of the ordinary relation of x having a larger population than y. Then, since Hong Kong has a larger population than Barcelona, $f(P(x,y))$ will include the ordered pair $\langle$Hong Kong, Barcelona$\rangle$, but not $\langle$Barcelona, Hong Kong$\rangle$ (or $\langle$Hong Kong, Hong Kong$\rangle$ or $\langle$Barcelona, Barcelona$\rangle$ either, since no number can be larger than itself). The sentence 'Hong Kong has a larger population than Barcelona' will be true, because the ordered pair $\langle f(a), f(b) \rangle$ is one of the ordered pairs assigned to the two-place predicate $P(x, y)$ by the interpretation function f. And 'Barcelona has a larger population than Barcelona' will be false, because $\langle f(b), f(b) \rangle$ is *not* on that list of ordered pairs that f assigns to $P(x, y)$.

An immediate consequence of this definition is that in a classical model, f is a *total* function: Every name is assigned some individual in D. However, in (most)[22] existentially free logics, f can be a *partial* function; that is, we allow some names in L to be assigned to no element in D. And a so-called inclusive logic relaxes the classical assumption that D is non-empty. A logic that relaxes both assumptions simultaneously is called 'universally free.'

In existentially free logics, we relax the classical assumption that the interpretation function be total. In uniqueness-free logics, we relax the assumption that the relation between linguistic items in L and (constructions in) D be a function, partial or otherwise. Instead, we model the relationship between names and elements of D as a *one-many relation*.[23] So, for example, using Camp's example of Fred's ant colony introduced in Section 2.1, the name 'Charley' in Fred's language signifies both Ant A and Ant B. We thus say that the interpretation relation (as opposed to interpretation function) for Fred's language holds of the ordered pairs $\langle$ 'Charley', Ant A $\rangle$ and $\langle$ 'Charley', Ant B $\rangle$. No other $x \in D$ satisfies $\langle$ 'Charley', $x \rangle$; 'Charley' only refers to the two large ants, not anything else. And of course, since every function can be characterized as a one-to-one relation, every classical interpretation function can also already be represented as an interpretation relation; that is, the notion of an interpretation relation generalizes that of an interpretation function.

Predicates in existentially free logics are treated exactly as they are in classical logic. This is because classical first-order logic already allows for predicates that are not true of any individuals, such as '5-sided triangle' or 'larger than itself.' One reason sometimes given for the superiority of existentially free logic over classical logic is that modern Fregean logic made genuine logical progress by dropping the Aristotelian assumption that every predicate is true of at least one thing;[24] existentially free logic simply completes that same progressive transition away from Aristotelian logic (Lambert & van Fraassen, 1972, p. 134–135), (Lambert, 2001, p. 262–263).

---

[22] The exception is the inner-domain/outer-domain semantics, discussed in Section 3.4.4.

[23] Priest (1995) also uses a one-many interpretation relation instead of an interpretation function.

[24] In other words, in Aristotelian logic, 'All Fs are G' logically entails 'Some Fs are G,' but this entailment does not hold in modern, post-Fregean logic.

In uniqueness-free logics, on the other hand, predicates are not treated exactly the same as in classical logics. If we allow names to be ambiguous, then there is no good reason to not let predicates be ambiguous as well. In a formal language where we use an interpretation relation instead of an interpretation function, a one-place predicate can be assigned two or more sets of elements from D. For example, recall the example of the ambiguous predicate 'warm-blooded' from Section 2.1. The interpretation relation would hold between the predicate for 'warm-blooded' and exactly three sets: the set of endothermic organisms, of tachymetabolic organisms, and of homeothermic organisms. In general, in a language that relaxes the uniqueness assumption, an n-place predicate can signify two or more sets of ordered pairs from D^n.

Finally, as mentioned above, a logic free of both existence and uniqueness assumptions for its terms will be called a 'generally free logic.' So, a model that provides a formal semantics for such a language will be called a 'generally free model.' Let us summarize the model theory more formally.

Four basic types of models

- **Classical Model:** $M = \langle D, f_I \rangle$, where
  - D is the domain of individuals, and
  - the interpretation function f_I assigns
    - (i) to every name in language L, exactly one element of D, and
    - (ii) to each n-ary predicate in L, exactly one set of ordered n-tuples from D^n
- **Existentially Free Model:** $M^E = \langle D, f_I^E \rangle$, which is exactly like a classical model, except the interpretation function f_I^E need *not* assign every name in L an individual from D.
- **Uniqueness-Free** (or Multiply-Signifying) **Model:** $M^U = \langle D, R_I^U \rangle$, where
  - D is the domain (exactly as above), and
  - R_I^U is a binary, (possibly) one-many *relation* between
    - (i) each name of L and (possibly many) elements of D, and
    - (ii) between each n-ary predicate and (possibly many) sets of ordered n-tuples from D^n
- **Generally Free Model:** $M^G = \langle D, R_I^G \rangle$, which is exactly like a uniqueness-free model, except the interpretation relation R_I^G need not hold of *every* name in L. That is, a generally free model allows for names c such that no $x \in D$ satisfies $R_I^G(c, x)$.

There is one more type of model that will be important in what follows: a *restricted model* (M^R). It is the most natural way of formally capturing the neutral semantics, but it also serves as an intermediate construction for the negative and one type of positive semantics as well. A restricted model is essentially a model that treats all non-univocal names and predicates as if they signified nothing, that is, as if they have no semantic contents at all. Every generally free model has exactly one associated restricted model, but in general the same restricted model can be generated from differing generally free models. What I called above an 'existentially free model' is already a restricted model. So if our language only has empty names, but no ambiguous terms, then the model for that language is already a restricted model. However, if our language has ambiguous names or predicates, so that the corresponding model uses an interpretation relation instead of an interpretation function, then we do not yet have a restricted model. We construct a restricted model from a generally free model as follows:

Restricted model (M^R)

The **Restricted Model** M^R built from the generally free model $M^G (= \langle D, R_I^G \rangle)$ is an ordered pair $\langle D, f^R \rangle$, where D is the same domain as in M^G, and f^R is the (possibly partial) function that meets the following two conditions:

- (M^R 1) For each singular term s, if R_I^G assigns s exactly one object $a \in D$, then $f^R(s) = a$; otherwise $f^R(s)$ is undefined.
- (M^R 2) For each n-ary predicate P, if R_I^G assigns P exactly one set of ordered n-tuples $T \subseteq D^n$, then $f^R(P) = T$; otherwise $f^R(P)$ is undefined.

In other words, the restricted model discards the information in M^G concerning which elements of D ambiguous names denote, and which sets of n-tuples in D^n ambiguous predicates signify. In exchange for this loss of information, we get a (partial) function in place of an interpretation relation.

There are two more items to add to the list of shared preliminaries. First, many free logics add to the language L a special one-place predicate for attributing (unique) existence to an individual, most commonly symbolized as '$E!(x)$'. '$E!(b)$' is true if 'b' refers to exactly one element in the domain D. If b refers to nothing in D, then '$E!(b)$' is false. If the language contains an interpreted identity predicate '$=$,' then '$E!$' can be defined in terms of it:

$$E!(x) =_{\text{def}} \exists y (x = y) \tag{E!}$$

The predicate '$E!(x)$' cannot be defined without '$=$' (Meyer, Bencivenga, & Lambert, 1982).

If this book were only about existentially free logics, we would leave the matter there. However, we are also examining logics with ambiguous names, such as 'Charley,' which refers to both Ant A and Ant B. Every undergraduate logic student is taught that the standard translation of the natural language sentence 'Cairo exists' into first-order logic is '$\exists x(x = \text{Cairo})$.' But note that this symbolization says, in effect, that there is at least one *and at most* one (thing identical to) Cairo. That is, '$\exists x(x = \text{Cairo})$' could perhaps be more perspicuously be rendered into English as 'Cairo exists *uniquely*,' or even 'There exists exactly one Cairo.'

So the natural question to ask at this point is: Does Charley exist? It is clear that '$\exists x(x = \text{Charley})$' is false, so if we use the canonical translation into a first-order language, then 'Charley exists' is false too. For some, this consequence may be welcome and intuitive.[25] However, for others, it will not be. For although neither Charley nor Atlantis exist in the same way you or I do, the case of Charley intuitively seems somewhat different from the case of Atlantis – especially to someone sympathetic to a positive semantics. For example, Charley (in some sense) plays a role in chains of causes and effect networks in the actual world, in a way that Atlantis and Santa Claus do not. And Charley is spatiotemporal in a way that Atlantis and Santa are not (Charley will have two spatiotemporal locations, instead of the usual single one – but that is different from having *no* spatiotemporal location, like Atlantis). One might object that Charley's causal effects are completely reducible to the causal effects of Ant A and Ant B; but many things we think exist in a completely typical way are completely reducible to other, more basic things too. So a supporter of a positive semantics might worry that the cases of ambiguity and empty names were being illegitimately collapsed, if 'Charley' and 'Atlantis' were assigned identical semantic statuses.

Thus one might hold that the question 'Does Charley exist?' should not be interpreted as equivalent to asking whether '$\exists x(x = \text{Charley})$' is true, for the latter involves a uniqueness claim that we need not think of as present in the former. Questions of existence and of uniqueness are standardly kept separate in mathematical proofs; perhaps they should be similarly kept apart for names as well. This can be done by introducing a special, interpreted predicate into our language, 'E' (without the '!'):

---

[25] For example, in *Metaphysics I*, Aristotle says: "[T]o be is to be one" (1003b23).

(E) '$E(t)$' ('t exists') is true in a generally free model $M^G (= \langle D, R_I^G \rangle)$ iff there exists at least one element $a \in D$ such that $R_I^G(t, a)$ holds; '$E(t)$' is false otherwise.

Thus, 'E(Charley)' is true, while '$E!$(Charley)' is false. But 'E(Atlantis)' is still false. So this predicate '$E(x)$' gives us a way to distinguish between the cases of Charley and Atlantis, and thus ambiguity is kept conceptually separate from non-existence.

The second shared preliminary concerns how to handle definite descriptions, phrases of the form 'The F,' symbolized as $\imath x F(\ldots x \ldots)$. As mentioned above on page 17, one motivation for free logic is that, from a linguistic point of view, definite descriptions appear to be singular terms, but Russell's theory of definite descriptions denies that they are. So a free logic should allow for definite descriptions to be singular terms that fail to uniquely refer to anything existing. All theories of definite descriptions take into account the possibility of the predicate F failing to be satisfied by exactly one existing thing. But in the context of uniqueness-free logics, we also need to take into account the possibility that the predicate F itself is ambiguous. The first two conditions below cover the standard cases; the third is included to account for cases of ambiguous predicates.

Definite descriptions in a restricted model

Let $F(x)$ be a predicate with x free. Recall that f^R is the interpretation function for a restricted model (defined on p. 30).

(DDR 1) If the set $f^R(F(x))$ contains exactly one member $b \in D$, then $f^R(\imath x F(x)) = b$.

(DDR 2) If the set $f^R(F(x))$ contains no members, or more than one member in D, then $f^R(\imath x F(x))$ is undefined.

(DDR 3) If the set $f^R(F(x))$ is undefined, then $f^R(\imath x F(x))$ is also undefined.

Note that (DDR 2) makes both 'The present king of France' and 'The big ant in Fred's ant colony' undefined. And even if there is exactly one animal currently in my kitchen, and that animal is a cat, (DDR 3) makes 'The warm-blooded animal in my kitchen' undefined as well (since 'warm-blooded' is ambiguous).

3.2 Neutral Semantics

The characteristic feature of a neutral semantics is that every atomic sentence containing a defective singular term or predicate (i.e., a singular term or predicate that violates the Principle of Univocality) is neither true nor false. The guiding idea behind the neutral semantics is 'Garbage in, garbage out,' or as Lehmann (1994) puts it (specifically about existentially free logic), "No input, no output," where we think of the interpretation of a sentence as a function that takes the semantic values of singular terms and predicates as inputs, and outputs either *true* or *false* as an output. In David Kaplan (1990, p. 109)'s words, when someone utters a sentence with a confused term, "nothing whatsoever is being said." On the neutral semantics, a sentence containing a defective name or predicate is analogous to an arithmetical expression that involves dividing by zero: There can be no answer, only an error message stating that the quantity is undefined. Put less metaphorically, if a component of a grammatical sentence, such as a name or a predicate, fails to make the appropriate type of semantic contribution to a sentence, then that whole sentence 'inherits' the failure of that component, and the whole sentence can be neither true nor false.[26] (*True* and *false* are the two types of semantic value appropriate for a sentence, from the classical point of view.)

3.2.1 Truth in Restricted Models: Anti-satisfaction for Atomic Sentences

Let us characterize truth in a restricted model for atomic formulas. We say that a well-formed formula (wff)[27] ϕ is *defined in* M^R iff every (individual and predicate) constant occurring in ϕ is assigned a value by f^R.[28] (Variables count as defined: They are never ambiguous or non-referring.) If ψ is an atomic wff and defined, then the truth-value of ψ in M^R is determined in exactly the same way as classical models assign truth-values to atomic wff's, that is, a formula is true if every sequence of elements in the domain satisfies it, and false if no sequence satisfies it. However, this definition of falsity only holds for *defined* wff's: If a predicate P multiply signifies, then no sequence will satisfy an open formula $P(x)$ (since f^R does not assign anything to P). Similarly, even if a binary predicate F does not multiply signify, the open formula $F(x, c)$ will not be satisfied by any sequence, if c violates the Principle of Univocality. So, if we simply identified 'ϕ is false' with 'No sequence satisfies ϕ,' then all undefined

---

[26] As we shall see in Section 3.2.2, there is disagreement over whether, in a compound sentence with one truth-valueless component, the whole sentence is always truth-valueless, or only sometimes. This is the difference between the so-called Weak Kleene and Strong Kleene schemes.

[27] A *well-formed formula* is a grammatical sentence of L, or a string of characters that would be a grammatical sentence if constants were substituted for every free variable in that string. So for example '$\forall x F(x, y)$' is a well-formed formula, because even though it is not a sentence, it would become a sentence if a name were plugged in for y.

[28] I will use Greek letters ($\phi, \psi, \ldots$) for well-formed formulas, and capital roman letters ($A, B, \ldots$) for sentences, i.e., well-formed formulas with no free variables.

formulas would come out false. But in the context of free logics, we want to distinguish between sentences that are untrue because they are semantically defective, and sentences that are untrue because they are determinately false and semantically impeccable.

To solve this problem, we introduce the notion of *anti-satisfaction*,[29] in order to allow for the possibility that some sequences neither satisfy nor anti-satisfy a wff. Intuitively, just as a sequence satisfies a wff containing free variables if that sequence assigns values to the variables that make the wff true, a sequence anti-satisfies a wff if the assignment of values to variables makes the wff (determinately) false. More precisely, a sequence *s anti-satisfies* an atomic wff ϕ iff ϕ is defined and *s* does not satisfy ϕ. Finally, an atomic wff is false in M^R iff every sequence anti-satisfies it. We thereby maintain the desired distinction between sentences that are false and sentences that are truth-valueless: If P is a multiply signifying predicate, then the wff $P(x)$ is not satisfied by any sequence, but it is not *anti*-satisfied by any sequence either, so it cannot be true or false when bound by a quantifier.

Stating anti-satisfaction conditions for compound expressions is straightforward; Appendix 1 spells out anti-satisfaction conditions fully. But to motivate and explain those conditions, we should discuss the definitions of truth and falsity for compound *sentences*, when we allow some sentences to be neither true nor false; the next subsection addresses that issue.

3.2.2 Compound Sentences with Truth-Valueless Components

For a semantics for free logic to qualify as neutral, it only needs to count every atomic sentence containing a defective name or predicate as neither true nor false. That means that a semantics merely being neutral does not fix the truth-value of compound sentences containing a truth-valueless component. There are different options available for how to determine the truth-value of compound sentences that have at least one truth-valueless component. This is relevant not just to languages that involve empty and ambiguous terms, because there could be other reasons why a sentence might lack a truth-value, beyond failures of the Principle of Univocality. For example, some philosophers have

---

[29] This term was chosen in order to mimic the 'extension/ anti-extension' terminology used in work on partially-defined predicates. Some philosophers model vague predicates, e.g., 'bald,' as having both an extension (the set of definitely, determinately bald people) and an anti-extension (the set of people who are definitely, determinately *not* bald). But there could be some individuals who are not members of either set, i.e., the people who are 'in-between' being bald and being non-bald. This contrasts with the semantic treatment of a predicate in classical logic, where every individual either definitely does, or definitely does not, fall under that predicate.

Table 1 Comparison of weak/internal versus strong/external negation

(a) weak/internal negation		(b) strong/external negation	
A	$\neg A$	A	$\neg A$
T	F	T	F
F	T	F	T
N	N	N	**F**

suggested that sentences containing vague predicates, or making claims about future events that are not yet settled, should be thought of as neither true nor false. There are two separate issues: first, how to deal with the word 'not' ($\neg$), and second, how to deal with 'and' ($\wedge$) and 'or' ($\vee$). We discuss them in turn.

In classical logic, if a sentence is not true, then the negation of that sentence is true. When we allow our language to contain truth-valueless sentences, we can keep that principle, or discard it. If we keep it, the result is so-called external or strong negation: The negation of a truth-valueless sentence is true.[30] If, instead, we hew more closely to the 'No input, no output' principle motivating the neutral semantics, then the negation of a truth-valueless sentence will again be truth-valueless (analogously, $-\frac{1}{0}$ is just as ill-defined as $\frac{1}{0}$). And the semantics for negation for sentences that are true or false can and should stay the same as in the classical case. These two proposals for negation are summarized in Table 1, where 'N' abbreviates 'neither true nor false.' Here, 'N' does *not* denote a third truth value; rather, 'N' signifies the absence of any truth value.[31] The single difference between the two truth-tables is highlighted in boldface. Readers interested in negation of sentences without truth-values (or negation more generally) should consult Laurence Horn (1989).

A similar pair of proposals is available for conjunction ('and') and disjunction ('or'). Once again, one option is to declare every sentence containing a defective term truth-valueless; this is the Weak Kleene scheme. The other option appeals to the plausible principles that (i) if at least one component of

---

[30] Braun (1993) defends this proposal.

[31] In certain circumstances, people have proposed thinking of the 'N' of the truth-tables in this subsection as a third or 'intermediate' truth-value, in-between the truth values of T and F. For example, Jan Łukasiewicz introduced a third truth-value between T and F to represent the truth-value of sentences that are not determinately true or false, in particular, sentences making claims about what happens in the future that has not yet been determined. Łukasiewicz called these sentences 'possible.' If we assign truth to 1 and falsity to 0, then the possible or indeterminate sentences have the value $\frac{1}{2}$ (Łukasiewicz, 1970, p. 87–88).

Table 2 Comparison of Weak and Strong Kleene schemes for $\land$ and $\lor$

(a) Weak Kleene					(b) Strong Kleene			
A	B	$A \land B$	$A \lor B$		A	B	$A \land B$	$A \lor B$
T	T	T	T		T	T	T	T
T	F	F	T		T	F	F	T
T	N	N	**N**		T	N	N	**T**
F	T	F	T		F	T	F	T
F	F	F	F		F	F	F	F
F	N	**N**	N		F	N	**F**	N
N	T	N	**N**		N	T	N	**T**
N	F	**N**	N		N	F	**F**	N
N	N	N	N		N	N	N	N

a disjunction is true, then the whole disjunction is true, and (ii) if at least one component of a conjunction is false, then the whole conjunction is false. The core idea is that both (i) and (ii) hold regardless of the other components of the whole sentence. This generates the Strong Kleene scheme. These two proposals are spelled out in Table 2; again, all the differences between the two proposals are in boldface.

Combining this with our discussion of negation above, we now have four total proposals for the semantics of the sentential connectives 'and,' 'or,' and 'not' (for example, internal negation + Strong Kleene is one option). And if we make the standard identification of $A \rightarrow B$ ('If A, then B') with $\neg A \lor B$, then we will also have four proposals for the conditional ($\rightarrow$) and biconditional ($\leftrightarrow$) connectives.

We will not discuss here the advantages and disadvantages of each of these four semantic proposals for the sentential connectives. But I do wish to point out that there is not one obviously correct choice. If we are committed to the general idea of 'no input, no output,' which originally motivated neutral logic in the first place, then the combination of weak negation plus Weak Kleene looks best. However, on that proposal, there are no propositional[32] logical truths, that is, sentences that are true in every row of the associated truth-table, containing individual or predicate constants. For example, $F(a) \lor \neg F(a)$ is neither true nor false, when $F(a)$ itself is neither true nor false.[33] But many people believe

---

[32] The 'propositional' qualifier is necessary, because there are still first-order logical truths in any generalized free logic. For example, $\forall x \forall y (x = y \rightarrow y = x)$ will still be a logical truth, even under the truth-tables that allow for the most truth-valueless sentences, because there are no names or non-logical predicates in it. Variables always obey the Principle of Univocality.

[33] $F(a) \lor \neg F(a)$ also fails to be a logical truth under two other proposals under discussion, namely weak negation plus Strong Kleene, and strong negation plus Weak Kleene.

that there are at least some logical truths. (These trade-offs will be discussed at greater length in Section 5.1.)

We now have all the materials needed to define truth and falsity in M^R, given a particular choice of truth-tables for the connectives:

Truth in a restricted model

- If every sequence *satisfies* formula ϕ, then ϕ is *true* in M^R.
- If every sequence *anti-satifies* ϕ, then ϕ is *false* in M^R.
- Formula ϕ lacks a truth-value in M^R otherwise.

Finally, the truth-value of a sentence on a neutral semantics is simply whatever truth-value is assigned to that sentence by M^R, given a particular specification of truth-tables for compound sentences – with one possible exception. For reasons described in Section 3.4.1, a proponent of the neutral semantics might want '$\exists x(x = \text{Charley})$' and/or '$\exists x(x = \text{Zeus})$' to be false. If that is the case, then condition (AS$_=$ 1) described below (p. 40) should be added to the definition of satisfaction and anti-satisfaction for a neutral semantics.

3.3 Negative Semantics

If you find the idea of declarative sentences that are neither true nor false undesirable, but nonetheless want a logic that allows for names that violate the Principle of Univocality, then you should consider adopting a negative semantics. Given all the machinery we have seen earlier in this section, the core idea of negative semantics is easily stated: Every atomic sentence that is truth-valueless in M^R is false, on a negative semantics.

The restriction to atomic sentences is needed to avoid contradiction. Suppose atomic sentence A contains a defective name. Thus the sentence $\neg A$ will also contain a defective name. If someone held that *every* sentence containing a defective name was false, then (by any plausible truth-table for '$\neg$') A would have to be both true and false. (That said, as we will discuss in Section 3.4.3, some people think that the right way to deal with ambiguity is to allow some sentences to be both true and false.)

One distinctive feature of negative semantics is that it makes certain instances of $b = b$ false, such as 'Pegasus = Pegasus,' 'Charley = Charley,' and 'The current king of France = the current king of France.' Another trait of negative semantics is that it makes the language bivalent: Every grammatical sentence is either true or false, unlike in the neutral semantics. Thus we can simply use the classical truth-tables for compound sentences. This feature is not unique to negative semantics; it is also shared with the positive inner-domain/outer-domain semantics that we will see in Section 3.4.4. Further, the classical satisfaction conditions can be used for quantified sentences; that is, we do not have to separate anti-satisfaction from non-satisfaction, if we choose to use negative semantics.

3.4 Positive Semantics

Positive semantics for generalized free logics are characterized by allowing at least some atomic sentences containing non-univocal names or predicates to be true, for example 'Zeus = Zeus.' There are multiple ways to accomplish this. Accordingly, different positive semantics will differ over which sentences containing non-univocal names or predicates are true, and which are false. This section will present three leading proposals for positive semantics for generalized free logic. But first, we must discuss how to treat atomic sentences containing an interpreted identity predicate ('=').

3.4.1 Identity in Generalized Free Logic

In our above discussion of the neutral and negative semantics for atomic formulas (Sections 3.2 and 3.3), we did not need to introduce any special conditions for sentences containing an interpreted identity predicate. Neutral and negative free logics treat a sentence $a = b$, where at least one of a, b fails to uniquely refer, like any other atomic sentence: such a sentence will lack any truth-value on the neutral semantics, and will be false on the negative semantics. But under positive semantics, we must introduce specific conditions on identity, in order to prevent the semantics from classifying obviously false things as true, such as 'There is exactly one ant named "Charley" in Fred's ant colony,' or 'Zeus exists.' We can avoid these consequences by including an additional complication in our truth-definition for atomic sentences of the form $a = b$ in M^R.

If an atomic sentence A has the form $P(a_1, a_2, \ldots a_n)$, and P or any of the a_i are undefined, then A has no truth-value in a restricted model M^R. But what about atomic formulas of the form $t_1 = t_2$, where t_i is an singular term, that is, a name or a variable (or a definite description, if the language contains them)? This creates complications. Suppose you want to adopt a positive free logic that classifies 'Zeus = Zeus' as true. However, if one also accepts as semantically valid the classical rule of existential introduction ('b is F, therefore something is F'), then 'Zeus = Zeus' entails '$\exists x(x = $ Zeus),' that is, 'Something is identical to Zeus.' And that final sentence seems pretty clearly false (assuming the quantifier $\exists$ is existentially committing, which all free logics do). So we must construct our positive semantics so that '$\exists x(x = $ Zeus)' comes out false, while preserving the truth of 'Zeus = Zeus.'

The situation with ambiguous names is similar, though this similarity is not immediately obvious. Recall Camp's example of the name 'Charley' (which I will abbreviate as c). Does any element in D satisfy the open formula $x = c$? There are strong reasons to answer *no*.[34] If the domain of discourse is the set of ants in Fred's colony, then the only two plausible candidates in D are Ant A and Ant B. But, by symmetry, there is no reason whatsoever to pick one ant over the other. And if we say *both* ants satisfy $x = c$, then by transitivity of identity,[35] we would be forced to accept that Ant A = Ant B, which is obviously untrue.[36]

Furthermore, we cannot say that the set {Ant A, Ant B} satisfies $x = c$, since that set is not an element of D, and thus not a permissible value for x. One could respond: Create a new domain D' that contains the sets of the elements in D (the powerset of D, perhaps without $\emptyset$). The set {Ant A, Ant B} is of course then an element of D'. However, this semantic proposal creates a further problem: 'Charley' is no longer an ambiguous or confused term: It univocally refers to that set. And furthermore, if 'Charley' refers to that set, then certain sentences will come out true that no defender of positive semantics thinks are true, such as 'Charley is a set' and 'Charley is not an ant.' A similar problem would arise if we assigned the name 'Charley' to the mereological sum of Ants A and B: 'Charley' would not be ambiguous, and 'Charley has two heads' would be true, while 'Charley has six legs' would be false.[37]

The proposal to assign the name 'Charley' to the set {Ant A, Ant B} is very similar to one of Frege's suggestions for dealing with definite descriptions that fail to refer uniquely (Pelletier & Linsky, 2009), for example, 'the square root of nine'. Namely, if the predicate in a definite description applies to more than one individual, then the definite description refers to the set of all individuals that satisfy that predicate; so the referent of 'the square root of nine' would be the set $\{-3, 3\}$. For another example, the definite description 'the big ant in Fred's farm' would refer to the set {Ant A, Ant B} on this proposal. But this suffers from the same problem treating 'Charley' as referring to a unique set does: Since that set is not among the individuals in the domain that satisfies the predicate 'is an ant' (since sets are not ants), the sentence 'The big ant in Fred's farm is an ant' would not be true, contrary to (at least) the spirit of multiply

---

[34] See Ripley (2018, fn. 7) for the opposite view.

[35] Graham Priest's position is that '=' is not transitive, in a language with names that refer to more than one individual (Priest, 1995). Priest's semantics will be explained in Section 3.4.3.

[36] Elmar Unnsteinsson (2022, ch. 2) argues that we (who are unconfused) should attribute to Fred the implicit belief that Ant A = Ant B; but attributing beliefs to others for the sake of explaining their behavior is clearly distinct from our semantics making 'Ant A = Ant B' true.

[37] In plural logic, pluralities can be values of variables. However, in plural logics, plural variables (which range over pluralities) are distinct from individual variables (Yi, 2005). But the variable in, e.g., 'x is an ant' is of course an individual variable, not a plural one.

signifying positive free logic. Incidentally, this is one reason why one simple, natural proposal for a positive semantics for definite descriptions would not be adequate; we will see more below (p. 44).

Here is a final argument against taking anything to satisfy $x = c$. If something satisfies $x = c$, then (on any reasonable semantics) $\exists x(x = c)$ will be true. But 'There is exactly one (thing identical to) Charley' is wrong; that is precisely Fred's mistake. The canonical, textbook formalization of that last sentence in classical first-order logic is

$$\exists x[(x = c) \wedge \forall y(y = c \rightarrow x = y)].$$

But note that this is a logical consequence of $\exists x(x = c)$. Thus (by *modus tollens*) nothing satisfies $x = c$.

In short, there are good reasons to hold that *nothing* in the domain is identical to Charley.[38] So, if a generally free language contains an interpreted identity predicate, and we want to make both '$\exists x(x = \text{Zeus})$' and '$\exists x(x = \text{Charley})$' false, without also making 'Zeus = Zeus' and 'Charley = Charley' false, then we can add the following conditions to the definition of anti-satisfaction for atomic formulas:

(AS$_=$ 1) If ϕ has the form $t_1 = t_2$, and exactly one of t_1, t_2 is undefined in M^R, then every sequence s anti-satisfies ϕ in M^R.

(AS$_=$ 2) If ϕ has the form $t_1 = t_2$, and both of t_1, t_2 are undefined in M^R, then no sequence s satisfies or anti-satisfies ϕ in M^R.

As a consequence, in M^R, 'Charley = Charley' will remain undefined.

Before spelling out the details of the various positive semantics, it is worth mentioning how a proponent of a neutral semantics could think about these two anti-satisfaction conditions on identity. It is possible that someone committed to neutral semantics might say that 'Zeus exists' and 'There exists exactly one thing identical to Charley' are false, in which case they could add these two conditions to their definition of truth in M^R. But it is also conceivable that a neutral semantics proponent would prefer to adhere to the core 'No input, no output' principle motivating neutral semantics, and hold that sentences like 'Zeus exists' and 'There exists exactly one thing identical to Charley' are neither true nor false.[39]

---

[38] Proponents of the subvaluational logics described in Section 3.4.3 maintain these reasons are not good enough.

[39] Lehmann (2002, p. 234) considers the former view; Meyer & Lambert (1968) and Lehmann (1994, p. 325) endorse the latter view.

3.4.2 Supervaluational Semantics

The core idea behind the supervaluational semantics is fairly simple and straightforward; however, various complications are needed to make everything work out as desired. Because the supervaluational machinery is less complicated for ambiguous terms than it is for empty names, we begin with supervaluational treatments of ambiguity.

Supervaluations for ambiguous terms. Let us first consider the case of a sentence containing an ambiguous name or predicate, that is, a name that refers to more than one individual, or a predicate that refers to more than one set of individuals in the domain. To oversimplify things slightly, that sentence will be supervaluated *true* iff it is true on every uniform disambiguation, it will be supervaluated *false* iff it is false on every uniform disambiguation, and it will lack a truth-value if it is true on some disambiguations and false on others. (The official definition of 'supervaluation' is on p. 43 below.)[40] So for example, on this semantics, 'Charley is an ant' will be supervaluated true (since both Ant A and Ant B are ants), and 'Charley is over one meter long' will be supervaluated false (since Ant A and Ant B are both much shorter than one meter long). If we imagine a situation where Ant A is awake, and Ant B is asleep, then at that moment, 'Charley is awake' is neither true nor false, as is 'Charley is asleep.' Note that the definition of supervaluational truth above includes the modifier 'uniform.' This means that, in a particular formula, if there are multiple instances of the same ambiguous term, then every instance of that term is disambiguated in the same way. Otherwise, 'Charley = Charley' would not be supervaluated as true, for we could disambiguate the first occurence of the name 'Charley' in that sentence as Ant A, and the second 'Charley' as Ant B, so that this mixed (i.e., non-uniform) disambiguation would be false. Allowing mixed disambiguations would result in a semantics that assigns truth-values in a way that is much closer to the neutral semantics, when the non-univocal terms appear more than once in a single sentence.

This supervaluational semantics 'saves' all the propositional classical logical truths. For example, every sentence of the form $F(b) \vee \neg F(b)$ is true, regardless of which element(s) in the domain b refers to, whereas in the classical context b must refer to one individual for a sentence of this form to be true. It also saves some first-order logical truths (though of course not all): 'Charley = Charley' comes out true on this semantic proposal, because Ant A is identical

---

[40] Whether we should count being supervaluated as true, i.e., being supertrue, as true simpliciter is a matter of debate in metaphysics and philosophy of language. Nicholas J. J. Smith (2016) argues that supertruth cannot be truth. Nothing said in this section depends on which position is taken in this debate.

to itself, and Ant B is identical to itself, and there are no other disambiguations of 'Charley' besides those two ants.

At this point, one should object that the supervaluational semantics delivers the wrong verdicts about certain sentences. In particular, no matter whether 'Charley' is assigned to Ant A or Ant B, the sentence 'There is exactly one ant identical to Charley' ($\exists x(x = c)$) will be true. But as we saw in the previous subsection, there are good reasons to think that sentence is false: no ant is identical to Charley. This potential problem is why so much time was spent in Section 3.4.1, discussing the special anti-satisfaction conditions that should be added for sentences containing '=.' This problem is solved by requiring that a supervaluation must always respect the assignment of truth-values to sentences that M^R makes over the truth-values assigned in a disambiguation – and (AS$_=$ 1) guarantees that $\exists x(x = c)$ will be false in M^R.

Let us spell this out more formally. We begin with the notion of a model that is a 'complete disambiguation,' that is, a model that assigns exactly one of the multiple extensions to each multiply signifying term. For example, if a language has exactly three multiply signifying terms, and the first term has two extensions, the second has five extensions, and the third has twelve, then there will be a total of $2 \times 5 \times 12 = 120$ complete disambiguation models for this multiply signifying model. We can capture this basic idea model-theoretically in the notion of a complete disambiguation of a multiply signifying model.

Complete disambiguation models

$M^d = \langle D, f^d \rangle$ is a *complete disambiguation model* of a multiply signifying (or 'uniqueness-free') model $M^U = \langle D, R_I \rangle$ iff:

(M^d 1) $R_I(a, f^d(a))$, where a is any individual constant,
(M^d 2) $R_I(P, f^d(P))$, where P is any n-ary predicate, and
(M^d 3) f^d is a total function.

To continue with our example of Fred's ant colony, there are two complete disambiguation models: In M_1^d, 'Charley' refers only to Ant A, and in M_2^d 'Charley' refers only to Ant B. Now, Field holds (in our terminology) that a sentence containing multiply signifying terms is true in M^U if it is true in each M^d constructable from that M^U.

However, this cannot be right. For $\exists x(x = c)$ is true in every disambiguation: In the first disambiguation $f_1^d(c) =$ Ant A, so $\exists x(x = c)$ is true in M_1^d, and in the second disambiguation $f_2^d =$ Ant B, so $\exists x(x = c)$ is true in M_2^d as well. However, we saw earlier that this sentence should not be true when c is multiply signifying.[41]

To avoid this problem, we can follow the strategy used by earlier supervaluation proposals for existentially free logic. The basic idea is that the truth-values assigned by the restricted model M^R trump the truth-values assigned by any disambiguation model M^d built on top of it. We characterize notions of *truth* and *falsity in M^d with respect to M^R*:

Truth in a complete disambiguation

(M^d **w.r.t.** M^R 1) If the formula ϕ has a truth-value in M^R, then the truth-value of ϕ in M^d-w.r.t.-M^R is the truth-value of ϕ in M^R.

(M^d **w.r.t.** M^R 2) If the formula ϕ has no truth-value in M^R, then the truth-value of ϕ in M^d-w.r.t.-M^R is the truth-value of ϕ in M^d.

Now we can finally define truth on a supervaluation (i.e., supertruth) in M^U:

Supertruth in a multiply signifying model

A wff ϕ is *supertrue* (resp. *superfalse*) in M^U iff ϕ is true (resp. false) in M^d-w.r.t.-M^R, for every M^d of M^U.

For example, $\exists x(x = c)$ will be superfalse (in the imagined M^U), because even though that sentence is true in every complete disambiguation model, it is false in the restricted model M^R (and the condition (M^d w.r.t. M^R 1) makes the truth-value assigned by M^R (false) override the fact that the sentence is true in every disambiguation). And $c = c$ and 'Charley is an insect' will be supertrue, because they are neither true nor false in M^R, but both are true in every complete disambiguation. And any sentence that has no truth-value in M^R, and is true in some disambiguations and false in others, will be neither supertrue nor superfalse.

There is one more complication concerning an interpreted identity predicate. Many pet owners give their pets nicknames, in addition to the pets' 'official' names. We can imagine Fred, the owner of the ant colony, sometimes refers to Charley using the name 'Chuck,' and other times using 'Charles,' as well as the original 'Charley.' Intuitively, it seems 'Charley = Chuck' and

---

[41] An analogous issue arises in the supervaluational treatment of vagueness. A vague predicate neither determinately applies nor determinately fails to apply to each element in the domain. However, in every precisification, every predicate's precisified extension either determinately applies or fails to apply to each element.

'Chuck = Charles' should be true. However, they will not be true on the above semantics; rather, they will be truth-valueless. Anti-satisfaction condition (AS$_=$ 2) makes them truth-valueless in M^R, and they will be true on some disambiguation models (namely, those models where 'Charley' and 'Chuck' are both assigned to the same ant) and false on others. At first glance, there is an obvious solution to this problem: Re-write the satisfaction conditions so that $a = b$ is true when a and b each multiply-refer to the same set of individuals, that is,

$$a = b \text{ is true in } M^R \text{ (based on } M^U) \text{ iff } \{x|R_I(a,x)\} = \{x|R_I(b,x)\}.$$

This would achieve the desired effect of making 'Chuck = Charley' true.

However, imposing this condition has the following consequence: Every identity statement involving two empty names would be true. For example, 'Pegasus = Zeus = Atlantis' would be true. Interestingly, this is a direct consequence of one of the stronger theories of positive free logic used for languages containing definite descriptions. Specifically, this logic is known as FD2, and its distinguishing trait is the following:

$$(\neg E!(t_1) \wedge \neg E!(t_2)) \rightarrow t_1 = t_2 \tag{FD2}$$

for any singular terms t_1, t_2 (including definite descriptions).[42] It is clear that, in a language with multiply referring singular terms, FD2 should not hold. For presumably, if Fred confused two of the other non-large ants in his colony, and called them by the name 'Andrea,' we should not say 'Charley = Andrea' is true.

If we consider 'Pegasus = Zeus' to be a problem, then we could fix it by only applying the above identity condition when a and b both refer to at least one thing:

(Positive satisfaction for = in M^R) $a = b$ is true in M^R (based on M^U) iff $\{x|R_I(a,x)\} = \{x|R_I(b,x)\}$, *and neither set is empty.*

This principle will not be assumed in what follows.

Finally, there is not yet an established supervaluational theory for definite descriptions in languages containing ambiguous terms; this remains an open area for research. Here is one difficulty. For example, suppose someone sympathetic to a positive supervaluational semantics wanted to construct a semantics in which 'Charley = The big ant in Fred's farm' is true. If they simply followed the satisfaction clause for '=' just above, then we would get:

---

[42] The logic FD2 results from adding the above to 'Lambert's Law'; see 66 below.

(Positive satisfaction for $\imath$ and $=$ in M^R) $a = \imath y P(y)$ is true in M^R (based on M^U) iff $\{x|R_I(a,x)\} = \{x|R_I(\imath y P(y),x)\}$.

This immediately raises the question of what satisfies $R_I(\imath y P(y),x)$. Given that we are trying to make 'Charley = The big ant in Fred's farm' true, the natural answer is: Every individual in the domain of M^U that satisfies P. In other words, $\imath y P(y)$ multiply refers to each of the individuals in the domain that satisfy P. This does not require adding anything to the model M^U: We can compute what satisfies $R_I(\imath y P(y),x)$ from $R_I(P,\Phi)$, and the latter is already given as part of the multiply signifying model. (Notice that this type of multiple signification does not require the language to have any multiply signifying basic components; that is, this kind of multiple signification can appear in a classical model.) And in our example, that would be Ant A and Ant B.

A problem arises when we combine this seemingly natural idea with another natural, and quite weak idea: Frege's only axiom for definite descriptions (Morscher & Simons, 2001, p. 21).

$$c = \imath x(x = c) \qquad \text{(Frege's $\imath$-axiom)}$$

for any name c. And this generates a problem, for we now have: 'The thing identical to Charley = Charley.' And whereas R_I (on our above proposal) associates two semantic values (Ant A and Ant B) with 'Charley,' it associates nothing with 'The individual identical to Charley' (Section 3.4.1 gives the reasoning).[43] In addition to this problem, things become even more complicated when we allow for definite descriptions with multiply signifying predicates, for the definite descriptions have to then be relativized to particular complete disambiguation models. In Section 4.2.2, the discussion of theories of definite descriptions for positive existentially free logics will highlight some other important differences between the existentially-free cases and the uniqueness-free cases; theories of descriptions for uniqueness-free languages remains an open research area.

Supervaluations for existentially free logic. One might initially think that it would be simple to re-purpose the supervaluational machinery earlier in this subsection to handle empty names. After all, an existentially free model is mathematically equivalent to the restricted models we used to discuss ambiguity. One might then take a cue from the *Science of Logic* §133, where Hegel claims that "pure nothing is . . . the same as pure being," since being and nothing

---

[43] Lambert (1972, p. 189–190) notes an analogous problem with Dana Scott's theory of definite descriptions.

both lack any specific, distinguishing characteristics. Following this line of thinking, we would take empty names to be maximally ambiguous, so to speak. Instead of a name like 'Charley,' which refers to only two elements of the domain of discourse, we treat 'Zeus' and 'Vulcan' as referring to *every* element of the domain. As a result, 'Vulcan = Vulcan' would be logically supertrue, since no matter what element of the domain we assign to the name 'Vulcan,' that element will be identical to itself. Similarly, 'If Vulcan is a planet, then Vulcan is a planet' and 'Vulcan is a planet, or it is not a planet' would be supertrue as well. And 'Vulcan = Zeus' would *not* be supertrue, since some complete disambiguation models would not assign the same element of the domain to both 'Vulcan' and 'Zeus.' This is all good news for someone who finds the idea of a positive semantics appealing.

However, as it stands, this proposal will not work as a semantics for existentially free logic. Recall that one of the key markers distinguishing free logic from classical logic is that the following are valid in classical logic, but not in free logic:

($\forall$-**Elimination**) $\forall x F(x)$, therefore $F(a)$
($\exists$-**Introduction**) $F(a)$, therefore $\exists x F(x)$

However, on the supervaluational proposal as described thus far in the present subsection, both of these are valid. For ($\forall$-Elimination), if every element in the domain is F, then whichever element the completion model assigns the empty name a to will necessarily be F as well. And ($\exists$-Introduction) would be valid too, since if we have picked an arbitrary element from the domain to assign to the empty name a, then whenever that element is F, then $\exists x F(x)$ must be true as well. So as it stands thus far, the supervaluational proposal described above looks more appropriate for classical logic than for a (positive) free logic.

Free logicians who want to use a supervaluational semantics recognize that ($\forall$-Elimination) and ($\exists$-Introduction) should not count as valid. So they use a model called a 'completion model' (or more briefly just a 'completion'), which is similar but not identical to a complete disambiguation model. A completion model starts from an existentially free model, that is, a model whose interpretation function is partial over the individual constants: Not every name is assigned an element of the domain. A completion model will 'fill in the blanks' of the existentially free model. Thus far, it does not differ from a complete disambiguation. The key differences are that, in a completion model, there is a completion domain D^c that contains the original base domain D as a proper subset, and the interpretation function for the completion model can assign elements of D^c to empty names, and the extensions of n-ary predicates can involve elements from D^c, whereas non-defective names must be assigned to elements of D.

> ## Completion models
>
> $M^c = \langle D^c, f^c \rangle$ is a *completion model* of an existentially free model $M^E = \langle D, f^E \rangle$ iff:
>
> (M^c1) D^c is non-empty, and $D \subset D^c$
> (M^c2) For any predicate P, $f^E(P) \subset f^c(P)$.
> (M^c3) If f^E is defined at an individual constant b, then $f^c(b) = f^E(b)$.

Note that ($\forall$-Introduction) and ($\exists$-Introduction) are still logically valid, if we supervaluate over such completion models. Without any further semantic tweaks, both entailments will be truth-preserving in every completion of every existentially free model. There are two ways in the literature to prevent ($\forall$-Introduction) and ($\exists$-Introduction) from being logically valid, in a supervaluational setting. The first and more common way is to change the semantics for the quantifiers: Let $\forall$ and $\exists$ range over D only, not over the whole D^c. Then both ($\forall$-Introduction) and ($\exists$-Introduction) will have a completion model where their premise is true but their conclusion is false. To see this for ($\forall$-Introduction), let every element of D be in the extension of F (i.e., $f^c(F) = D$), so that $\forall x F(x)$ is true, but let a be an empty name assigned to an element in D^c that is not in the extension of F (i.e., $f^c(a) \in (D^c - D)$), so that $F(a)$ is false. For a completion model where ($\exists$-Introduction) is false, let $f^c(a)$ again be an element of $D^c - D$ and $f^c(a) \in f^c(F)$, so that $F(a)$ is true. Further suppose that the extension of F contains no elements of D (i.e., $f^c(F) \cap D = \emptyset$), so that $\exists x F(x)$ is false.

Ermanno Bencivenga proposes a slightly different strategy to prevent ($\forall$-Introduction) and ($\exists$-Introduction) from being supertrue. He uses the same definition of completion models, but he does not alter the usual semantics for the quantifiers, that is, quantifiers still range over every element of a completion model (so 'all' really means *all* of the elements, and not just a proper subset of them). Bencivenga uses a two-stage process for supervaluating a sentence, which is similar to the notion of truth in M^d-w.r.t.-M^R that we saw a few pages ago; here, it will be truth in M^c-w.r.t.-M^E. First, determine all the truth-values in the 'base' model M^E. Each of these truth-values always trumps any truth-values assigned via supervaluating on the completion models. For example, if there is a sentence that is made true in the base model, but is false in some completion models, then that sentence is simply true, not truth-valueless. So let us apply this to ($\forall$-Introduction) and ($\exists$-Introduction). Suppose we have a existentially free model M^E, with at least one empty name a. Further suppose that in this model, $\forall x F(x)$ is true, that is, every member of D is in the extension of F, but $F(a)$ has no truth-value, since a is undefined. When we make completion models that assign a referent to a, that referent will have to be in $D^c - D$. And in some completion models, $f^c(a) \in f^c(F)$; in those models, both the premise and conclusion of (∀-Introduction) are true. And in other completion models, $f^c(a) \notin f^c(F)$; in those models, the premise and conclusion of (∀-Introduction) are both false. So there is no completion model where the premise of (∀-Introduction) is true, but its conclusion is not (this is what distinguishes Bencivenga's method from the one described in the previous paragraph). As a result, we cannot identify 'supertrue' with 'truth in all completion models,' since that would make (∀-Introduction) truth-preserving, violating the fundamental spirit of free logic. This is why the two-stage evaluation process is necessary. If a sentence has a truth-value in the base model, that truth-value always overrides anything the chorus of completion models says. On this two-stage semantics, (∀-Introduction) is not logically valid. There are models M^E where $\forall x F(x)$ is true because it is true in the base model M^E, but $F(a)$ is not evaluated as true, because it is not true in all completion models.[44]

3.4.3 Subvaluational Semantics

This subsection presents two related positive semantics. These two semantic proposals are only intended to apply to multiply signifying terms; they were not designed to address languages with empty names. On both, a sentence is true iff it is true on *at least one* complete disambiguation (though, as we shall see, these disambiguations are different from the ones we just saw for the supervaluational semantics).

Lewis-Priest semantics.   Imagine you know that I am spending my lunch break sitting next to the river that runs through our town. Someone then asks you 'Is Greg at the bank?'. You do not know if this person is asking if I am at the strip of land bordering our local river, or instead if I am at a financial institution where I could deposit checks and make withdrawals. So you reply 'Well, yes and no.' This is a perfectly normal response in everyday conversation, though on its face your answer appears contradictory. This response seems completely unexceptional to a typical English speaker, because saying 'Yes and no' in reply is conventionally used to signal to the question-asker that the hearer thinks the question is ambiguous. That is, the responder is communicating that if the sentence is interpreted in one way, the answer is 'yes,' but if it is interpreted it in another legitimate way, the answer is 'no.' Now, if one thinks 'Yes and no' is the best way to answer this question, then one might naturally also think that the declarative sentence 'Greg is at the bank' should be both true and false.

---

[44] For the technical details of this two-stage assignment of truth-values, see Bencivenga (1981) and Bencivenga (2002).

Thus, ambiguity can be used to motivate a relatively mild version of *dialetheism*, the view that a single sentence can be true and false. This is often called a 'truth-value glut' (contrasted with a 'truth-value gap,' when a sentence has no truth-value). And if we keep the standard principles that the negation of a true sentence is false, and the negation of a false sentence is true, then there can be a sentence A where both A and its negation $\neg A$ are true (and also both false). Thus, dialetheism allows for true contradictions. I called this a mild or weak form of dialetheism, because unlike standard, stronger dialetheism, one could accept all of the above and still maintain that there are no *propositions* (i.e., the semantic contents of sentences) that are both true and false simultaneously. On this weaker form of dialetheism, only *sentences* can be true contradictions; propositions cannot. For it is reasonable to claim that a single sentence can be ambiguous between two propositions, even if one thinks that propositions themselves cannot be ambiguous: The sentence 'Greg Frost-Arnold is at the local bank' is ambiguous between (i) the unambiguous proposition that I am at the land bordering the river running through our town, and (ii) the unambiguous proposition that I am at the local financial institution. David K. Lewis (1982) uses the fact that ambiguity is a feature of everyday life to motivate the use of truth-value gluts, and thereby to motivate using a relevant logic. Graham Priest (1995, 2016) does the same, but for first-order logic, whereas Lewis only deals with the propositional case. See also Ripley (2018).

Once sentences that have more than one truth-value are allowed, we must also revisit the sentential connectives. The standard approach, advocated by Priest, is to keep the classical characterizations of the connectives unchanged. Thus, for example, consider the conjunction $A \wedge B$. Suppose A is both true and false, while B is true only. Classically, a conjunction is true iff both conjuncts are true. Thus, $A \wedge B$ is true. But classically, a conjunction is false if at least one of the conjuncts is false. And in the sentence under consideration, A is false (as well as true), so $A \wedge B$ is false too. So the conjunction $A \wedge B$ is both true and false, when one conjunct has both truth-values, and the other conjunct is just true.

At this point, you might think that Lewis and Priest's proposal can be framed using the concept of a complete disambiguation introduced earlier, as follows. A sentence A is true iff it is true on at least one complete disambiguation model, and it is false iff A is false on at least one complete disambiguation model. As it turns out, this does not accurately capture the Lewis-Priest semantics. The reason is that they allow for "mixed disambiguations" (Lewis, 1982, p. 439), that is, when the same expression appears more than once in a single sentence, the different instances of that expression can be assigned different semantic values. Here is why they permit mixed disambiguations. Imagine a situation in which Ant A is eating, but Ant B is not. Consider the following argument:

1. Charley is eating
2. ¬(Charley is eating)

3. Charley is eating ∧ ¬(Charley is eating)   ∧ **Intro:** 1, 2

On the Lewis-Priest semantics, the first premise is true, since Ant A is eating, and the second premise is also true, since Ant B is not eating. (Both premises are also false as well.) However, there is no uniform disambiguation model in which Ant A is both eating and not eating, and there is also no uniform disambiguation model in which Ant B is both eating and not eating. So then the conclusion is not true in any uniform disambiguation model, in which case the proof rule of ∧-Intro fails. Because Priest and Lewis want ∧-Intro to be a valid rule, their response to this situation is to allow mixed disambiguations: In a sentence where the same ambiguous expression appears twice, the two tokens of the expression can be semantically assigned different disambiguations. Thus, the conclusion in the above argument is true and false: It is true, because if we assign Ant A to 'Charley' in the first conjunct, and Ant B to 'Charley' in the second conjunct, then both conjuncts are true. Thus, there is a mixed disambiguation in which $A \wedge \neg A$ is true. So the ∧-intro rule is saved by allowing for mixed disambiguations. Note that allowing for mixed disambiguations will make 'Charley = Charley' both true and false (likewise for 'Charley ≠ Charley').

McLeish semantics.   Finally, suppose you do not want to accept either the truth-value gluts of the Lewis-Priest semantics, or the truth-value gaps of the supervaluational semantics, but you still want some sentences containing defective terms to be true (and others false), that is, you want a positive semantics. Christina McLeish (2006) has proposed a semantics which does exactly that. Loosely speaking, McLeish's proposal combines Lewis and Priest's truth-definition with the supervaluational one. Lewis and Priest treat truth and falsity symmetrically: To repeat what was said above, a sentence is true iff it is true in at least one complete mixed disambiguation, and false iff it is false in at least one complete mixed disambiguation. McLeish's proposal, in contrast, handles truth and falsity asymmetrically: It uses the same truth-definition that Lewis and Priest do, but says a sentence is false iff it is false on *all* complete disambiguations. Thus, on McLeish's semantics, there are no sentences that are both true and false, distinguishing her proposal from Lewis and Priest's. But there are also no truth-valueless sentences created by ambiguities, thereby distinguishing it from the supervaluational semantics, which declares a sentence neither true nor false if it is true on some disambiguations but not on others. On first glance, McLeish's semantics might appear to be the best of both worlds, especially if one is reluctant to accept non-standard truth-value assignments, that is, one wants to avoid truth-value gaps and gluts. But as we shall see later (in Section 4.3.3), this view has its own implausible consequences. In particular, the logical rule of ∧-Introduction is no longer valid.

3.4.4 Inner-Domain/Outer-Domain Semantics

The two species of subvaluational semantics just discussed are specifically for terms that refer to too much, not terms that refer to nothing. The inner-domain/outer-domain semantics, the topic of this subsection, is the converse: It was designed to handle empty names, but (as we will see) does not naturally apply to ambiguous terms.

After looking at the outcomes of the supervaluational semantics, someone who was drawn to positive semantics might think the supervaluational semantics 'does not go far enough,' in the sense that there are some sentences about things that do not actually exist that the supervaluational semantics classifies as truth-valueless, but should nonetheless be true. For example, one might want to say that 'Gregor Samsa is a giant insect' or 'Vulcan is a planet' are true, even though neither Gregor Samsa or Vulcan exist (Dumitru & Kroon, 2008, p. 106–108). Similarly, one might think 'Zeus is one of the Ancient Greek gods' is true, even though 'Zeus exists' and 'Ancient Greek gods exist' are both false (Bacon, 2013). But on the supervaluational semantics, 'Vulcan is a planet' and 'Zeus is an Ancient Greek god' will not be true (or false).

The central technical idea of inner-domain/outer-domain semantics is simple. A classical model, as we have seen, consists of a domain and a interpretation function ($M = \langle D, f_I \rangle$). The inner-domain/outer-domain semantics begins from a classical model, and splits the domain into two mutually exclusive and exhaustive subdomains, called the inner and the outer domains ($D = (D_i \cup D_o)$, and $(D_i \cap D_o) = \emptyset$). Intuitively speaking, the elements of the inner domain are intended to represent entities that exist, whereas the elements of the outer domain represent non-existent items like Zeus and Vulcan. Inner-domain/outer-domain model theory does not use the notion of a restricted model. This semantics is exactly the same as the classical semantics, with only one exception: The quantifiers *only* range over the elements of the inner domain, not the elements of the outer domain. And if the language contains an existence predicate, that predicate is satisfied by all and only the elements of the inner domain.

This modification to the classical quantifier semantics can generate the desired truth-value assignments described in the paragraph before last. For if $f_I(\text{'Zeus'}) \in D_o$, then $\exists x(x = \text{Zeus})$ is false. And if every other Ancient Greek god is also in the outer domain along with Zeus, then 'Ancient Greek gods exist' will be false as well. However, the predicate 'Ancient Greek god' can still apply to the elements in the outer domain intended to represent Zeus, Hera, and the rest: f_i('Zeus'), f_i('Hera'), ... $\in f_i$('Ancient Greek god'). Because the only difference between the inner-domain/outer-domain semantics and classical model theory is confined to the quantifiers, in an unquantified sentence (like 'Hera is an Ancient Greek god'), the extension of a predicate does not 'care' whether an element is in the inner domain or the outer one. So the sentence 'Zeus is an Ancient Greek god who does not exist – and neither do any of the other Ancient Greek gods' can be true, if we use the inner-domain/outer-domain semantics, instead of the supervaluational semantics.

Might we use an inner-domain/outer-domain semantics for ambiguous terms, as well as empty names? The suggestion is not absurd on its face. To use the example of Fred's ant colony again, we can imagine that Ant A and Ant B are both elements of the inner domain, and that there is a third element, in the outer domain, which is supposed to represent Charley. So far, so good. But the difficult question is: What, if anything, is the relation between the third entity representing Charley in the outer domain, and the two elements Ant A and Ant B in the inner domain? It seems that the traits of Ants A and B should constrain Charley's traits in at least some ways: Charley is not as independent from the actual world as Zeus is. For example, it seems plausible to hold that 'Charley is an insect' is true because Ant A and Ant B are both insects, a fact determined by facts about the inner domain, that is, what is actual, whereas, for example, 'Zeus is Hera's spouse' is not made true by anything actual except an admittedly fictional story. But if we go that route, then it seems we have just re-invented the supervaluational semantics, but with added complications (namely the outer domain). Perhaps something would be gained over the supervaluational semantics, either philosophically or logically, from introducing a third element into the outer domain to represent a conflated object. But I do not see one. And other initially plausible suggestions for what that third object would be, such as the set whose only members are Ant A and Ant B, or the mereological fusion of them, would run into the same problems described earlier in Section 3.4.1. But perhaps it is possible; I consider this an open question. And Krista Lawlor considers it an important question:

> In supervaluing, we give up on understanding the confused belief, [because] Fred's ontological commitments involve one big ant . . ., not two. Our assignment of truth and falsity to Fred's beliefs rests on our ontology, not Fred's. . . . In a very clear sense we give up on understanding Fred, in favor of using him . . . as an instrument . . . for detecting the facts as we understand them. (Lawlor, 2007, p. 153)

Meinongianism. The inner-domain/outer-domain semantics is related to another venerable philosophico-logical topic: Meinongianism. Graham Priest, who has worked to revive Meinongian views based on the work of Richard Routley (1980), identifies the minimal core of this doctrine as 'Noneism' (Priest, 2016, xxvii):

(Noneism) Some things do not exist.

Put slightly differently: Not all properties are existence-entailing. Priest (and others, including Berto [2013] and Nolt [2010 §5.5]) maintain that Noneism is more commonsense and plausible than the (Parmenidean/Quinean) view that everything exists. It should be clear why Noneism fits nicely with the inner-domain/outer-domain semantics: The 'things that do not exist' in the Noneist thesis are (represented by) the elements in an outer domain.

Of course, for the doctrine of Noneism to be coherent, we cannot (contra introductory logic texts) read the quantifier 'some' in the statement of Noneism as the standard existential quantifier $\exists$ of classical logic: 'There exists something that doesn't exist' is plainly incoherent. So the Noneist introduces a new quantifier for 'some' ($\mathfrak{S}$) which does not carry existential assumptions, and ranges over the entire domain, the outer domain as as well as the inner. As a result, 'Some things do not exist' is true in a model just in case there is at least one element in the outer domain. The characteristic Noneist slogan can be precisely expressed as $\mathfrak{S}x\neg E!(x)$ in a language with a unique existence predicate, and as $\mathfrak{S}x\neg\exists y(x = y)$ in a language with identity. There is a corresponding universal quantifier ($\mathfrak{A}$) that ranges over the whole inner and outer domains as well. The semantics for the new quantifiers are precisely the classical ones, over the entire domain $D = D_i \cup D_o$. Note that we can define the old classical quantifiers in terms of their Meinongian counterparts, provided we have an existence predicate:

- $\exists x F(x) \Leftrightarrow \mathfrak{S}x(E!(x) \wedge F(x))$
- $\forall x F(x) \Leftrightarrow \mathfrak{A}x(E!(x) \rightarrow F(x))$

So anything that can be said in a classical language can also be said in this Meinongian language. (However, we cannot define the new, extended quantifiers in terms of the old, standard ones.)

Now, a question any philosophically inclined person would have about Noneism and the inner-domain/outer-domain semantics is: What exactly are the things in the outer domain? What determines what is included in the outer domain, and what is not? An answer to this question goes beyond the bare statement of Noneism, but many people will not be satisfied with Noneism as a brute, unexplained assertion. Meinong himself, as well as many Neo-Meinongians, generally argue for the group of non-existing items to be as large as it can be, without creating disastrous consequences (and different people have different views of what counts as a disaster). For one consideration motivating these thinkers is that the Problem of Empty Names (Section 2.3.1) is a real problem: If I am thinking or talking about Pegasus, then there must be *something* that I am thinking or talking about. I am not thinking of *nothing* (as I would be during a dreamless sleep, for example); the thing I am thinking of just happens to lack the property of existence. And human beings are capable of thinking about all sorts of things, existing or not. We are even arguably able to think about things that are not just non-existent but impossible, since we make claims like 'Penrose's triangle is impossible,' which states that a particular thing cannot have the property of existence. If the justification for (Noneism) is that humans can think about lots of non-existent things, then the set of non-existent things, that is, the population of the outer domain, will be everything coherently conceivable. And given any set of properties, humans can posit and entertain some object that has those properties.[45] This is called the (naive or unrestricted) 'characterization principle' or 'comprehension principle': For any property or set of properties P, there is an item or thing b_P (possibly in the outer domain) having those properties, that is, $P(b_P)$ (Berto, 2013, p. 86).

Unfortunately, this simple, naive characterization principle leads to consequences even Meinongians find unacceptable. First, this principle guarantees the existence of every object. Meinongians stress, contra the philosophical orthodoxy, that existence is just one property among others: Some things have it, others do not. But if that is true, then it can appear in instances of the unrestricted characterization principle: The principle guarantees not only an object that has the properties of both being golden and a mountain (which Meinongians are happy with), but also a thing that has the three properties of being golden, a mountain, and existent. And even Meinongians do not want to endorse the obviously false claim that a golden mountain actually exists. Second, the unrestricted characterization principle allows us to prove literally anything (Priest, 2016, p. xix). Let A be an arbitrary sentence. Now consider the (admittedly artificial) property $x = x \wedge A$. The unrestricted characterization principle guarantees that there is an object with that property, call it c. So $c = c \wedge A$ is true, and A immediately logically follows from that sentence. Since

---

[45] This way of phrasing the Meinongian idea is perhaps misleading, for it makes Meinongianism sound completely dependent on the contours of human psychology. Whether our limited brains ever happen to think of a particular item is not essential: We can think of the possible 'objects of thought' as preexisting human cognition, waiting to be discovered by human minds.

A was arbitrary, this shows that endorsing the unrestricted characterization principle allows you to prove anything.

Philosophers working in the Meinongian tradition have offered several ways to avoid this problem.[46] One route restricts the set of properties that can occur in the characterization principle (Parsons, 1980). In particular, the property of existence is disallowed; this prevents the Meinongian from accepting that a golden mountain, or greatest natural number, actually exists. The key difficulty with this approach is providing a principled distinction between properties that are allowed in the (restricted) characterization principle and those that are not, that is not merely a post hoc rationalization contrived for no reason other than saving Meinongianism from apparent counterexamples (Priest, 2016, p. 83). A second way Meinongians have responded to the two problems described in the previous paragraph is via what Berto calls 'modal Meinongianism.' This accepts a unrestricted comprehension principle, but instead of holding that $P(b_P)$ is true in our world, that is, in the actual world (as the original version does), instead holds the much weaker claim that it is true at *some* world (Berto, 2013, p. 141), (Priest, 2016, p. 84). So 'The existent golden mountain exists' is true, just not at our world. And if your Meinongianism allows you to think about impossible objects like the round square, your semantics will need to include impossible worlds along with possible ones. Priest (2016) and Berto (2013) both pursue this project in detail.

Looking over the options for a positive free semantics canvassed above, one might like the bivalence of the inner-domain/outer-domain semantics, but feel hesitant about allowing non-existent things into the (outer) domain; conversely, one might like that the supervaluational semantics avoids any non-existent things in its (base) domain, but dislike that it allows for truth-value gaps. As a result, one might wonder whether it would be possible to have the best of both worlds, namely, a positive semantics that is both bivalent and does not contain elements meant to represent non-existent things in its technical machinery. Aldo Antonelli (2000, 2007) has proposed just such a positive semantics. I will not present the whole apparatus here, but the central idea can be explained informally. Antonelli's semantics adds information to the interpretation function for names and predicates, so that, in effect, the interpretation function will encode the information that makes, for example, 'Zeus is a Greek god' come out true, and 'Zeus is a horse' come out false. For each ordered n-tuple of names, and every n-place predicate in the language, the interpretation function determines

---

[46] Berto (2013) provides a comprehensive survey of these various Meinongian solutions. He includes the proposal, omitted here, of Zalta (1983), whose core idea is that the 'is' in 'Atlantis is a city' means something different from the 'is' in 'Buenos Aires is a city.'

whether that n-tuple creates a true sentence when combined with that predicate – regardless of whether all those names refer or not. Antonelli himself calls this maneuver "somewhat artificial" (like other positive free semantics) (Antonelli, 2007, p. 71), but it does show that it is technically possible to have a bivalent positive free logic that does not need anything to represent non-existent individuals. The price is dissociating true predications from the central, intuitive idea of things having properties.

4 Proofs and Logical Consequence

Thus far, we have characterized the differences between free logics and classical logic in terms of truth and reference: What happens when we allow names in our language that refer to nothing? Or to more than one thing? But free logics can also be distinguished from classical logics in terms of what proof steps are allowed in a valid argument. There are certain steps that classical logic permits that free logics do not, namely classical ∀-elimination (also called 'Universal Instantiation') and ∃-introduction (also called 'Existential Generalization'). Free logics do not simply eliminate these two rules entirely; rather, they weaken those two classical rules. In effect, the two free-logic versions of these rules are just the classical rules plus the additional premise that the individual at issue exists. Some changes to the proof rules for '=' are also needed, as well as rules involving the existence predicate '$E!$'. Section 4.1 first explains why those rules (typically) fail in free logics, then 4.2 presents alternative proof rules for existentially free logics, followed in 4.3 by rules for uniqueness-free logics, and how they compare to the existentially free ones.

Proof systems for free logics have been presented in many of the major types: axiomatic formulations, the sequent calculus, tableaux/trees, et cetera. The discussion in this section will use Fitch-style natural deduction, in part because it is popular in introductory logic instruction (and this Element's intended audience includes people who have taken only a first-order logic course), and because those other formats are widely available in other overviews of free logics. It should be noted at the outset that there is no such thing as 'the proof rules of positive free logic' or 'the proof rules of negative free logic.' Rather, there are multiple, non-equivalent but similar formal proof systems.[47]

---

[47] Norbert Gratzl (2010, p. 331) writes "there is no particular formal system called 'the' negative free logic, but there is a whole family of such systems." And Indrzejczak & Zawidzki (2021, fig. 2) list five different (positive and negative) proof systems.

4.1 Classical Proof Rules

In classical logical systems, it is legitimate to deduce 'Pat is hungry and angry' from the generalization 'Everyone is hungry and angry.' The principle underwriting this deduction is formalized as the proof rule of 'universal instantiation' or ∀-elimination:

Classical ∀-elim:

$$1.\ \forall x \phi(\ldots x \ldots)$$
$$2.\ \phi(\ldots [b/x] \ldots) \qquad \text{∀ Elim: } 1$$

where b is any name, ϕ is any well-formed formula, x is free in $\phi(\ldots x \ldots)$, and $[b/x]$ means that the name b has been substituted for all occurrences of the variable x in ϕ.

In terms of proofs, the characteristic difference between classical logic and existentially free logic is that the above principle holds unrestrictedly in the former, but not in the latter. Matters are slightly different in uniqueness-free logics; Section 4.3 will examine how ambiguous names relate to the classical ∀-elim rule. We saw in Section 1 that allowing empty names into a language makes classical ∀-elimination invalid on the various semantics, but let us briefly recap how each of the various semantics allow the sentence 'Everything is hungry' to be literally true without 'Santa Claus is hungry' also being true. For the inner-domain/outer-domain semantics, there are models in which every individual in the inner domain falls under the extension of the predicate 'hungry,' that is, 'Everything is hungry' is true, but the extension of 'hungry' does not include anything in the outer domain. Similarly for a supervaluational semantics: In some completion models, the referent of 'Santa' is neither in the domain of the base model, nor in the extension of 'hungry.' So 'Santa is hungry' will be neither supertrue nor superfalse, in models where 'Everything is hungry' is true. If $\phi(\ldots [b/x] \ldots)$ is atomic, then in negative semantics it will always be false, and in neutral semantics it will always be truth-valueless, even in models where $\forall x(\ldots x \ldots)$ is true.

Additionally, in classical logic, the step from 'Pat is hungry and angry' to 'Someone or something is hungry and angry' is valid, and so is every argument with the same form. This is called 'existential generalization' or ∃-introduction:

Classical ∃-intro:

$$1.\ \phi(\ldots b \ldots)$$
$$2.\ \exists x \phi(\ldots [x//b] \ldots) \qquad \text{∀ Elim: } 1$$

where '$[x//b]$' means that x is substituted for some or all occurrences of b in ϕ. In most[48] existentially free logics, this classical proof principle does not hold unrestrictedly. It is easy to see why in the case of the inner-domain/ outer-domain positive semantics. For a concrete example, let b be 'Vulcan' and $\phi(x)$ be 'x is a planet closer to the Sun than Mercury.' Putting this in terms of models, $f_I(b)$ will be an element the outer domain. Furthermore, it will also be in the extension of $f_I(\phi)$. Thus, the sentence $\phi(b)$ will be true. But because no elements of the inner domain are in the extension of ϕ, $\exists x \phi(x)$ is false. Furthermore, this rule is invalid for supervaluational free semantics as well: As before, let b be 'Vulcan.' Now let $\phi(x)$ be 'x = Vulcan.' On the supervaluational semantics, 'Vulcan = Vulcan' is true, but '$\exists x(x = \text{Vulcan})$' is false. (This example works for the inner-domain/outer-domain semantics too.)

This classical rule of $\exists$-intro is also invalid in generalized negative free logic, and in neutral free logics that use 'external' or 'strong' negation. Here is why. Suppose the individual constant b does not uniquely refer. In negative free logic, $F(b)$ must be false, so $\neg F(b)$ is true. In neutral free logic, $F(b)$ is truth-valueless, but applying external negation to a truth-valueless sentence results in a true sentence (see Table 1, p. 35). So, on both semantics, $\neg F(b)$ is true. Applying the classical rule of $\exists$-intro to this true sentence results in $\exists x \neg F(x)$. But the extension of the predicate F could be the entire domain D (i.e., $f_I(F) = D$), in which case $\exists x \neg F(x)$ would be false. (For example, let the predicate F mean 'is identical to itself,' i.e. $F(b)$ means the same thing as $b = b$.) Thus, the classical rule of $\exists$-intro can take us from a true claim to a false one, in positive existentially[49] free logics, negative free logic, or a neutral free logic with external negation.

What about neutral free logics with internal negation? This question is worth asking, in part because the combination just considered of external negation and neutral semantics is not really conceptually compelling. The main motivation for adopting a neutral semantics (Lehmann's 'No input, no output' principle) seems like it would also push one toward internal negation and away from external negation. To answer this question, we need a to draw a distinction between two notions of validity that perfectly coincide in classical logic. Classically, every sentence is either true or false (and not both). When that holds, the following two characterizations of validity are equivalent:

---

[48] This qualification is necessary, because the classical $\exists$-intro rule is truth-preserving for neutral logics, as long as (i) the semantics assigns '$\exists x(x = \text{Atlantis})$' no truth-value, and (ii) negation is internal, not external (for this distinction, see Table 1 on p. 35).

[49] As we shall see in Section 4.3.2, the two proof rules of $\forall$-elim and $\exists$-intro also fail to hold in some species of uniqueness-free logics, but not in all.

(Forward-truth-preserving [FTP] validity) An argument is FTP-valid iff in every situation where all the premises are true, the conclusion is also true.

(Backwards-falsehood-preserving [BFP] validity) An argument is BFP-valid iff in every situation where the conclusion is false, at least one premise is also false. (This is equivalent to forward non-falsity preservation.)

These two types of validity are equivalent in the classical case because there, 'true' is equivalent to 'not false.' However, if we allow sentences that are neither true nor false (like any neutral semantics, or a supervaluational positive semantics), then these two ways of characterizing validity can come apart. For a supervaluational example, consider again the argument we saw on p. 50:

> 1. Charley is eating
> 2. ¬(Charley is eating)
>
> 3. Charley is eating ∧ ¬(Charley is eating)   ∧ **Intro:** 1, 2

Suppose Ant A is eating, but Ant B is not. Then this argument fails to be backwards-(super)falsehood preserving, since the conclusion is superfalse, but neither premise is superfalse. However, it is still forward-(super)truth preserving: no argument of the form $F(a)$, $\neg F(a)$, *thus* $F(a) \wedge \neg F(a)$ can have supertrue premises (and a conclusion which is not supertrue). For another example, consider the argument from $F(b)$ to $\exists x F(x)$, where $F(b)$ is atomic. In a neutral free logic, this is forward-truth preserving, but not backwards-falsehood preserving. It is forward-truth preserving because the only way $F(b)$ can be true is if both b and F are defined, and the referent of b falls under the extension of F. When those two conditions are met, at least one thing in the domain is F, thereby guaranteeing the truth of the conclusion. However, this argument form is *not* backwards-falsehood preserving. Let b be an empty name, and let the predicate F apply to no individuals. Then $F(b)$ will be neither true nor false, but $\exists x F(x)$ will be false. So, returning to our original question, 'Is classical ∃-intro valid in a neutral semantics with internal negation?', we can see that the answer is 'Yes and no': *Yes*, insofar as it is forward-truth preserving, but *no* insofar as it is not backwards-falsehood preserving. However, note that in a *negative* free logic, this example will be backwards-falsehood preserving, since $F(b)$ will be false, given that b is an empty name. And generally, the two notions of validity coincide for negative free logic, and for positive free logics using the inner-domain/outer-domain semantics, since both of these are bivalent. The situation is complicated for languages that allow truth-value gluts. In terms of the cases we have discussed, Lewis' preferred logic (R-Mingle) is both FTP and BFP, whereas Priest's preferred Logic of Paradox is FTP but not BFP (Dunn, 2000, p. 11). The situation is similar for the other classical rule that fails in free logics, $\forall$-elimination. In neutral free logics, it is not forward-truth preserving, but it is backwards-falsehood preserving. To show this, consider the $\forall$-elimination argument scheme:

$$\left|\begin{array}{l} \forall x \phi(\ldots x \ldots) \\ \hline \phi(\ldots [b/x] \ldots) \end{array}\right.$$

This is not forward-truth preserving: Imagine a situation where everything in the domain satisfies $\phi(\ldots x \ldots)$. The premise will then be true. But if b does not denote, then the conclusion will be neither true nor false. (This is immediate if $\phi(\ldots [b/x] \ldots)$ is atomic.) But this argument form is backwards-falsehood preserving, even on the Strong Kleene scheme (in which some sentences containing empty names can have truth values: e.g., $A \wedge B$ is false, when A is false and B is truth-valueless). If b is defined, this is immediate: If the individual b refers to does not satisfy $\phi(\ldots x \ldots)$, then the universal quantification of that open formula for x will be false. What about the case where $\phi(\ldots [b/x] \ldots)$ is false, and b is undefined? In that case, the components of $\phi(\ldots [b/x] \ldots)$ that do not contain b already determine the truth-value of that sentence (just as, on the Strong Kleene scheme, the falsity of A must already determine the truth-value of $A \wedge B$: The conjunction will be false, regardless of whether B is true, false, or neither). But if the truth-value of $\phi(\ldots [b/x] \ldots)$ is already determined by the b-free components of that sentence, then changing the components that contain b (including if we replace b with a bound variable and quantify over it) cannot change the truth-value of the resulting sentence (because vacuous quantification – in this case, over the b-free parts of the sentence – does not change truth-values). So if $\phi(\ldots [b/x] \ldots)$ is false, then $\forall x \phi(\ldots x \ldots)$ must be false too, regardless of whether b is defined or not.

4.2 Existentially Free Proof Rules

Although the classical versions of $\forall$-elimination and $\exists$-introduction do not hold in all existentially free logics, restricted or weakened versions of those two rules do hold. The classical rules are valid in classical logic because there, (i) the quantifiers range over everything that exists, and (ii) the name at issue refers to something that exists. Free logics keep (i) but drop (ii). What the weakened free-logic proof rules in effect do is require (ii) to be explicitly stated as a line in a proof, when one wants to use $\forall$-elimination or $\exists$-introduction. (As we shall see, for languages without an existence predicate or an identity predicate, a workaround can be devised, using subproofs.)

4.2.1 Proof Rules Shared by All Existentially Free Logics

The existentially free ∀-elimination rule takes the original, classical rule, and adds the requirement that the individual being instantiated exists:

Existentially Free ∀-elim:

> 1. $\forall x \phi(\ldots x \ldots)$
> 2. $E!(b)$
> 3. $\phi(\ldots [b/x] \ldots)$ ∀ **Elim:** 1, 2

where b is any name, referring or empty, and '$E!(x)$' formalizes 'x exists.' As mentioned in our earlier discussion about existence and identity in Section 3.1, if our language contains '=,' then premise 2 above can be replaced with $\exists x(x = b)$. Notice that, in a sense, this rule also functions as an elimination rule for E! (though only in a sense: The free ∃-intro rule will discharge existence-claims as well, so there is not a single E!-elimination rule). Also, note that this rule fulfills the basic free-logic goal of preventing arguments like 'Everything is hungry, therefore Santa Claus is hungry' from counting as valid.

What about languages that do not contain a predicate for 'E!' or '='? Proof rules become slightly more complicated, but they are still possible. Lambert and van Fraassen (1972, §4.5) make use of the fact that in free logics variables only range over the elements that exist; if we are working within a two-domain semantics, then variables can only range over the 'inner domain' (see also Wu [1988] and Hazen & Pelletier [2014, §2.2.5]). As first-order logic students learn, some proofs involve reasoning about arbitrary objects (specifically, the ∀-intro and ∃-elim rules require us to use arbitrary objects). These arbitrary objects are represented as boxed letters in the rules below. So, when reasoning about arbitrary objects within subproofs, the arbitrary object is represented by a (new) variable, to guarantee that we are talking about a unique and existent arbitrary object. The ∀-elim rule (in its classical form) can only be applied when working within a subproof in which the variable being instantiated by the rule is one of these special variables. This way of setting up the ∀-elim rule involves allowing lines in a proof to contain free variables. However, lines with free variables are only allowed to appear within subproofs.[50] Depicting this in a Fitch-style format:

---

[50] There are other ways; for example, instead of using variables for the arbitrary existing objects, we could introduce a new type of individual symbol that, by stipulation, can only refer to a unique existing object in the domain, and use that as our boxed letter, instead of a variable. For example, instead of x, y as in the main text, we could introduce boldface individual constants **a, b** that are guaranteed to refer to unique existing objects (Hardegree, 2016, §VII-14).

Existentially Free ∀-elim (no = or E!):

$$n. \boxed{y}$$

$$n + k.\ \forall x \phi x$$

$$\vdots$$

$$\phi[y/x] \qquad \forall\ \textbf{Elim:}\ n + k$$

provided y is free for x in ϕ.

There is a parallel free analog for the classical rule of ∃-introduction, which again is just like the classical rule except it adds the requirement that the individual at issue exists:

Existentially Free ∃-intro:

1. $\phi(\ldots b \ldots)$
2. $E!(b)$
3. $\exists x \phi(\ldots [x//b] \ldots)$ ∃ **Intro:** 1, 2

where again, we can substitute $\exists x(x = b)$ for premise 2, if the language contains '=.' And as above, it is also possible to introduce such a rule in languages that do not contain the predicates '=' or 'E!.'

Existentially Free ∃-intro (no = or E!)

$$n. \boxed{y}$$

$$n + k.\ \phi y$$

$$\vdots$$

$$\exists x \phi[x/y] \qquad \exists\ \textbf{Intro:}\ n + k$$

provided y is free for x in ϕ.

In a natural deduction system of proof, we need both an introduction and elimination rule for each logical symbol. Here are the other halves for the two rules introduced above:

Existentially Free ∀-intro

1. $E!(t)$

$$\vdots$$

$n.\ \phi(t)$

$n + 1.\ \forall x \phi(x/t)$ ∀ **Intro:** 1–n

Existentially Free ∃-elim

1. $\exists x \; \phi(x)$

   2. $\boxed{t} \; \phi[t/x] \wedge E!(t)$

   ⋮

   n. ψ

ψ **∃ Elim:** 1, 2–*n*

where *t* does not appear outside the subproof.

4.2.2 Rules Distinguishing Free Logics from Each Other

This section focuses on positive and negative free logics. Neutral logics will be mentioned in passing, but not discussed in detail. The reason for this is that less proof theory research has been done on them. There is only one formalization for which soundness and completeness has been proven (Lehmann, 1994). This one is given in Jeffrey-style tree rules (unlike the rest of the discussion here, which has been Fitch-style natural deduction rules), and its semantics adheres strictly to the 'No input, no output' principle (so, e.g., 'Zeus = Zeus' and '$\exists x(x = \text{Zeus})$' are both truth-valueless). There is currently no natural deduction or sequent calculus formulation of neutral semantics that is sound and complete;[51] this is an open area for research.

The rules presented in Section 4.2.1 hold in all varieties of existentially free logics. But of course, there are different species of free logic, and these are distinguished from each other in terms of which arguments are valid, and thus which proof-rules each system has. There are two related differences between positive and negative free logics. They differ over the proof-rules for the existence predicate and the identity predicate.

We saw on p. 58 that the classical ∃-intro rule is invalid in negative free logic. (Brief reminder why: Negative free logic declares 'Pegasus is identical to itself' false, which therefore makes 'Pegasus is *not* identical to itself' true; applying the classical existential generalization rule to that true sentence would yield the false sentence 'Something is not identical to itself,' $\exists x(x \neq x)$.) However, if the classical rule is applied to an *atomic* sentence in negative or neutral free logic, then the classical rule is forward-truth preserving in neutral free logic and fully valid (i.e., both forward-truth preserving and backwards-falsehood preserving) in negative free logic. (The example about Pegasus applied ∃-intro to a negated, and thus non-atomic, sentence.) That is,

---

[51] Pavlović and Gratzl (2021, p. 118) briefly discuss why there has been less proof-theoretical research done on neutral free logic, in comparison with positive and negative variants.

$$\left|\begin{array}{l} F(\ldots b \ldots) \\ \hline \exists x F(\ldots [x//b] \ldots) \end{array}\right.$$

is forward-truth-preserving in negative and neutral free logic, *if* $F(\ldots b \ldots)$ is atomic. This is because $F(\ldots b \ldots)$ is true only when b is defined, and falls under the extension of $F(\ldots x \ldots)$. So there must be something that is F. Karel Lambert calls this "perhaps the most important difference between negative and positive free logics" (Lambert, 2001, p. 266). It is also backwards-falsehood preserving in negative free logic, but *not* in neutral free logic (since even if there are no F's in the domain, $F(a)$ will be truth-valueless in a neutral semantics if a is an empty name).

To capture this difference, negative free logic contains the following rule, which positive free logic lacks:

Negative E!-Intro $\left|\begin{array}{ll} 1.\ F(\ldots b \ldots) & \\ 2.\ E!(b) & E!\ \textbf{Intro: 1} \end{array}\right.$

where $F(\ldots b \ldots)$ is atomic. (Recall that sentences of the form $a = b$ are atomic.) And if we apply the existentially free $\exists$-intro rule to lines 1 and 2 in the rule just above, we can derive $\exists x F(x)$. That is, the classically basic $\exists$-Intro rule $F(\ldots b \ldots) \vdash \exists x F(\ldots x \ldots)$ is a derived rule in negative free logic – but for atomic sentences only. In positive free logic, on the other hand, there is no E!-Introduction rule.[52] And for reasons similar to the preceding paragraph, in a neutral free logic, this rule is forward-truth preserving, but not backwards-falsehood preserving (unless the semantics makes $E!(b)$ truth-valueless, when b denotes nothing).

The second difference between positive and negative proof rules for existentially free logics is the rule for =-Introduction. Positive free logics simply use the classical rule:

Positive and Classical =-Intro $\left|\begin{array}{ll} \vdots & \\ t = t & = \textbf{Intro} \end{array}\right.$

for any term (name, variable, or definite description) t (some systems allow free variables to occur as lines of a proof, as we saw above). Negative and neutral

---

[52] Nils Kürbis (2021, p. 333–335) offers logical and philosophical reasons for leaving $E!$ undefined.

free logics, on the other hand, weaken this rule by (once again) requiring that the name refer to something that exists.

Negative and Neutral $=$-Intro

1. $E!(t)$
2. $t = t$ $=$**Intro:** 1

Finally, in another area of overlap, both positive and negative free logics use the classical rule for $=$-elimination, namely:

$=$**-Elim**

1. $F(\ldots b \ldots)$
2. $b = c$
3. $F(\ldots [c//b] \ldots)$ $=$ **Elim:** 1, 2

Thus we can prove the transitivity of identity (If $a = b$ and $b = c$, then $a = c$) in positive and negative free logics. In neutral free logics, this rule is forward-truth preserving, but not backwards-falsehood preserving, unless we declare $t_1 = t_2$ false when exactly one of the t_i does not univocally refer (which would violate the 'No input, no output' motivation of the neutral semantics). Let us look at two simple examples that use these rules, to see the rules in action. We can easily prove that $c = c$ and $E!(c)$ are equivalent in negative free logic:

1. $c = c$

2. $E!(c)$ $E!$ **Intro:** 1

3. $E!(c)$

4. $c = c$ $=$ **Intro:** 3

5. $E!(c) \leftrightarrow c = c$ $\leftrightarrow$ **Intro:** 1–2, 3–4

This equivalence does not hold in positive free logics, since there '$E!(\text{Zeus})$' is false, but 'Zeus = Zeus' still counts as true. This corresponds in the proof above to the fact that the positive proof rules cannot prove line 2 from line 1. Here is another example. Axiomatic formulations of both positive and negative existentially free logics typically include $\forall x E!(x)$ as an axiom. This sentence captures the idea that the quantifiers range over only the existing things (or as it is often phrased, 'The quantifiers have existential import'). This principle is derivable from the rules we have introduced:

1. $E!(t)$

2. $t = t$ $=$ **Intro**: 1 (Neg)

3. $\exists y(t = y)$ $\exists$ **Intro**: 1, 2

4. $\forall x \exists y(x = y)$ $\forall$ **Intro**: 1–3

And given that $E!(x)$ is defined as $\exists y(x = y)$, the final line of this proof is equivalent to $\forall x E!(x)$. (In line 2, the justification reads '1 (Neg)' because the $=$-Intro rule does not require a justifying line for positive free logic, but a justification is required in a negative free proof system.)

The final rules to present are rules for definite descriptions. All existentially free logics that allow for definite descriptions adopt what is called 'Lambert's Law,' which we capture here in the following two symmetric rules:

$\imath$-**Elim**

1. $c = \imath x \phi(x)$

2. $\forall x(\phi(x) \leftrightarrow x = c)$ $\imath$ **Elim**: 1

and its mirror image,

$\imath$-**Intro**

1. $\forall x(\phi(x) \leftrightarrow x = c)$

2. $c = \imath x \phi(x)$ $\imath$ **Intro**: 1

In an inner-domain/outer-domain semantics, we might expect a sentence like 'Sherlock Holmes = the detective living at 221B Baker Street, London' to be true. However, if Lambert's Law holds, then that sentence will not be true. For the name 'Sherlock' will be assigned to an individual in the outer domain, whereas the definite description 'the detective living at 221B Baker Street' will not be assigned to anything in the inner or outer domain. For, as always in free logics, the quantifiers $\forall$ and $\exists$ are existentially committing, so they range over the inner domain only. And as we can see in the two immediately preceding rules, Lambert's Law is framed in terms of $\forall$.[53] We obtain a negative free description theory by placing Lambert's Law in the context of the characteristic Negative E!-Intro rule (see p. 64), applied to the special case of definite descriptions. That is:

---

[53] Priest (2016, §4.6) presents a theory of descriptions that uses, instead of $\exists$ and $\forall$, the quantifiers $\mathfrak{S}$, $\mathfrak{A}$ which range over both the outer and inner domains (see p. 53). Priest's theory involves complications that we will not delve into here.

1. $\imath x\phi(x) = \imath x\phi(x)$
2. $E!(\imath x\phi(x))$ *E*! **Intro:** 1

This theory generates results close to Russell's theory in "On Denoting" (Burge, 1974), (Morscher & Simons, 2001, p. 22). For example, the sentence 'The present king of France = the present king of France' is assigned the value *false*.

The range of positive free description theories are myriad and complex. Lambert (2002) presents several of them, arranging them into a two-dimensional hierarchy of proof-theoretic strength. The two rules just above are the weakest (along one axis), and the system FD2 discussed on page 44 is the strongest. See Kürbis (2021) for a positive free description theory in an intuitionist logic.

Although Lambert's Law is the weakest of the viable existentially free description theories, it is violated in a language that contains multiply referring names and definite descriptions. For suppose, as a defender of a positive semantics would, that 'Charley = the big ant in Fred's colony' is true. If $\imath$-Elim were truth-preserving, then (i) every big ant would be identical to Charley, and (ii) everything identical to Charley would be a big ant. But (i) is false, because Ant A is not identical to Charley. ((ii) is vacuously true.) As I have mentioned before, there is not yet a positive semantics for definite descriptions in multiply signifying languages. This is one of the reasons: Even the weakest principle of existentially free description theory fails in multiply signifying languages.

Metatheory.   How do these proof rules relate to the semantics discussed in the previous section? Recall that a proof system is called *sound* with respect to a particular semantics if every proof is truth-preserving, and called (strongly) *complete* if every truth-preserving argument has a proof in that system. We will not prove soundness and completeness here. For the soundness and completeness of negative free logic, see Schock (1968). For a combined treatment of both negative and positive bivalent (i.e., inner-domain/outer-domain semantics) free logic, see Pavlović & Gratzl (2021). For an intuitionistic natural deduction system, see Troelstra & van Dalen (1988). For the soundness and completeness of a neutral free logic, see Lehmann (1994); we have not discussed Lehmann's proof system here, because it uses Jeffrey-style trees, instead of Fitch-style natural deduction. There is not yet a formulation of neutral free logic in a natural deduction format or in the sequent calculus. Bencivenga (1981) showed that the positive proof rules are sound with respect to supervaluational semantics. Logical consequence in supervaluational (i.e., non-bivalent) positive semantics, however, is *not* strongly complete (van Fraassen, 1966b, p. 491), and cannot be finitely axiomatized in a proof system (Woodruff, 1984); that is why the discussion in this subsection was restricted to *bivalent* positive free logic. That said, the positive proof rules are *weakly* complete with respect to supervaluational semantics, that is, every logical truth (i.e., sentence supertrue in all models) is a theorem of positive free logic (i.e., can be proved from zero premises) (van Fraassen, 1966a).

4.3 Uniqueness-Free Logical Consequence

Let us now turn to logical consequence and possible proof rules for languages that contain ambiguous or confused terms such as 'Charley.' This is far less studied and less developed than existentially free logics. This section proceeds via comparing uniqueness-free languages to the existentially free languages discussed in the previous section. Specifically: Do the same classical rules fail in the uniqueness-free case as in the existentially free case? And under the same circumstances? And what proof rules, if any, should be used to systematize the different uniqueness-free logics? There are interesting differences; for example, the classical proof-rules for ∀-elimination and ∃-introduction turn out to be valid on one plausible semantics, unless the language contains '=.'

4.3.1 Neutral and Negative Consequence

In Section 4.1, we saw the classical rules of ∀-elimination and ∃-introduction are not valid in existentially free logics. Is the same true of uniqueness-free logics? The ∀-elimination rule is also not truth-preserving for uniqueness-free languages, when the negative or neutral semantics is adopted. For example, in models where 'Everything is hungry' is true, 'Charley is hungry' will be false on a negative semantics, and truth-valueless on a neutral semantics. This same example shows that, on the negative semantics, ∀-elimination also fails to be backwards-falsehood preserving. However, just as in the existentially free case, on a neutral semantics ∀-elimination *is* backwards-falsehood preserving, even if the name being instantiated is ambiguous (see p. 60 for the argument).

What about the ∃-introduction rule? In uniqueness-free languages with the negative semantics, applications of this rule can take us from true premises to a false conclusion, and for exactly the same reasons as in the existentially free case. Suppose everything in the (non-empty) domain of quantification is an ant. Under the negative semantics, 'Charley is an ant' is false, so 'Charley is *not* an ant' is true. Applying ∃-introduction to this sentence yields 'Something is not an ant,' which is (by original supposition) false. In the neutral semantics, ∃-introduction is forward truth-preserving, but it is *not* backwards-falsehood preserving: In a model where 'Something is hungry' is false, 'Charley is hungry' will still be neither true nor false.

As mentioned at the end of Section 4.2, for negative and neutral existentially free logics, there are sound and complete proof systems. Now, negative and neutral uniqueness-free semantics are based on restricted models (M^R, see p. 30), which are almost identical to the existentially free models (M^E, see p. 29) used in semantics for neutral and negative existentially free logics. The only difference between restricted and existentially free models is that the latter models forbid undefined predicates, whereas restricted models allow them, since uniqueness-free languages allow predicates to be ambiguous. Thus, one might expect that the proof systems developed for neutral and negative free logics could carry over to the uniqueness-free cases. It turns out that this expectation is not met for neutral uniqueness-free languages, but it is for the negative uniqueness-free languages. Let us see why each of those two claims hold in turn.

First, let us show that there are sentences that are logical truths in neutral existentially free logic that are *not* logical truths in neutral uniqueness-free semantics. (And thus, there are arguments that are truth-preserving in existentially free, but not uniqueness-free, neutral logics.) The sentence $\forall x(F(x) \rightarrow F(x))$ demonstrates the claimed fact. For in a restricted model, though not in an existentially free model, F can be undefined. So in a M^R where F is undefined, the open formula $F(x)$ will not be satisfied or anti-satisfied by any sequence. And in (satisfaction-analogues of) both the Strong and Weak Kleene schemes, a conditional formula whose antecedent and consequent are both neither satisfied nor anti-satisfied is itself neither satisfied nor anti-satisfied. So $\forall x(F(x) \rightarrow F(x))$ will be neither true nor false in a M^R where F is undefined. In a neutral existentially free logic, in contrast, $\forall x(F(x) \rightarrow F(x))$ is a logical truth, since F must be defined.

Furthermore, since neutral existentially free logic is complete, $\forall x(F(x) \rightarrow F(x))$ is a theorem of neutral existentially free logic. Thus, this example shows that a proof system for neutral existentially free logic is not even weakly sound on neutral uniqueness-free semantics. So we cannot simply borrow without alteration the existentially-free proof systems to use the uniqueness-free proof systems. (These proof systems are complete on neutral uniqueness-free semantics, because every neutral existentially-free model is a restricted model.)

Now we can turn to logical consequence in negative uniqueness-free languages. Above, I asserted that an argument is valid in negative *existentially* free semantics iff it is valid in negative *uniqueness*-free semantics. Why? First, since every existentially free model is a restricted model, the right-to-left direction is immediate. So, we need to establish the left-to-right direction: for every assignment of truth-values to a set of formulas in negative uniqueness-free semantics, there is a existentially-free model that assigns exactly the same set of truth-values to that set of formulas. The basic idea is that, whenever a predicate is undefined in a negative restricted model, it will assign truth-values exactly as if it were a defined predicate that applies to nothing. And predicates that apply to nothing, that is, whose extension is empty, of course already appear in all types of models, including existentially free ones. And the negative semantics for existentially and uniqueness-free logics share exactly the same clauses for the truth of compound formulas (i.e., the same truth tables and satisfaction clauses). So every assignment of truth-values to a set of formulas in negative uniqueness-free semantics will be identical to an assignment of truth-values to that same set in negative existentially free semantics. Therefore, there cannot be an argument where (i) there is an M^R that makes the premises true and the conclusion untrue, yet (ii) in every M^E either the premises are false or the conclusion is true. In other words, we have the left-to-right direction we needed: Every argument valid on the negative existentially free semantics is also valid on the negative uniqueness-free semantics. With that fact in hand, we can immediately infer that negative uniqueness-free logic has a sound and complete proof system, since negative existentially free logic has one (as we saw on p. 67): They share the same one.

4.3.2 Positive Consequence: Supervaluational (and Related) Semantics

If we adopt a positive semantics for uniqueness-free languages, then, in contrast to existentially free languages, the ∃-introduction and ∀-elimination rules appear sound at first glance. Why? Consider ∃-introduction first. Suppose the domain is all the ants in the colony, and Fred says 'Charley is eating.' If that sentence is true on the positive supervaluational semantics, then Ant A and Ant B are both eating. And if Ants A and B are eating, then 'Something is eating' is obviously true – so ∃-introduction appears valid. The ∀-elimination rule likewise looks to be valid: Imagine Fred, looking at his colony, says 'Everyone is eating.' If this is true, then both Ants A and B must be eating; and if that is the case, then on the supervaluational semantics 'Charley is eating' is true.

This intuitive illustration of the apparent validity of ∀-elimination and ∃-introduction in uniqueness-free languages with a positive semantics ignores a crucial distinction. Specifically, it ignores the difference between what the vagueness literature calls 'global' and 'local' consequence,[54] or what I will

---

[54] Varzi (2007) provides a nice taxonomy and comparison of various species of global and local consequence in the setting of supervaluational treatments of vagueness.

call here 'supervaluational' and 'semi-classical' consequence.[55] The core distinction is the following: Supervaluational validity forbids supertrue premises combined with a superfalse conclusion, whereas semi-classical validity forbids any disambiguation model that makes all the premises true (w.r.t. M^R), but the conclusion false (w.r.t. M^R).

(Supervaluational validity) An argument is *supervaluationally valid* $=_{\text{def}}$ for every M^U and each of its associated M^d's, if each premise is true in every M^d-w.r.t.-M^R, then the conclusion is also true in every M^d-w.r.t.-M^R.

(Semi-classical validity) An argument is *semi-classically valid* $=_{\text{def}}$ for every M^U and each of its associated M^d's, there is no M^d-w.r.t.-M^R in which all the premises are true, but the conclusion is not.

Every semi-classically valid argument is supervaluationally valid, but not conversely (since 'All Fs are Gs' entails 'If everything is F, then everything is G,' but not conversely).

To illustrate these two concepts, note that 'Charley is an ant' entails 'Something is an ant' both semi-classically and supervaluationally. In each complete disambiguation where 'Charley' is assigned to an element of the domain that is an ant, 'Something is an ant' will be true in that disambiguation (w.r.t. M^R). That is, 'Charley is an ant' semi-classically entails 'Something is an ant.' Also, in every multiply-signifying model in which 'Charley is an ant' is true on all disambiguations w.r.t. M^R, 'Something is an ant' will also be true on all disambiguations w.r.t. M^R. In other words, 'Something is an ant' supervaluationally follows from 'Charley is an ant.' To make the difference between these two types of validity clearer, consider an example where the two concepts of consequence come apart. Consider the argument 'Charley is eating, thus every big ant is eating.' This is supervaluationally valid, but not semi-classically valid. Suppose Ant A is eating, but Ant B is not. That situation describes an M^d-w.r.t.-M^R in which the premise is true (assuming f_I('Charley') = Ant A in this model) and the conclusion is false. But note that in that situation the premise is not supertrue, so this case does not invalidate the argument.

As mentioned on p. 67, Bencivenga (1981) showed that positive existentially free logic is sound with respect to supervaluational consequence. Now, positive existentially free logic uses non-classical versions of $\forall$-elim and $\exists$-intro. But

---

[55] Free logicians (following van Fraassen) call this distinction 'supervaluational' vs. 'classical' consequence (van Fraassen, 1966b), (Woodruff, 1984). But I find the name 'classical consequence' potentially misleading, since free logics using this semantics make the *classical* versions of $\forall$-elimination and $\exists$-introduction invalid. Thus I shall call this type of consequence 'semi-classical.'

in the first paragraph of this subsection, it appeared that the *classical* ∀-intro and ∃-elim rules are sound w.r.t. positive semantics. As it turns out, those two classical rules are unsound in a uniqueness-free language with an interpreted identity predicate, but they are both sound if the language does not contain '=.'

In the next subsection, I will first show that the classical rules of ∀-elim and ∃-intro are unsound in a language with identity using supervaluational consequence. Thus, they are unsound using semi-classical consequence as well, since (as explained above) every semi-classically valid argument is supervaluationally valid too. Then, in the following subsection, I show that classical ∀-elim is sound in languages without an identity predicate using semi-classical consequence (thereby showing that it is sound using supervaluational consequence as well).

Languages with identity: Classical ∃-intro and ∀-elim fail. In uniqueness-free languages with an interpreted identity predicate, classical ∃-introduction and ∀-elimination both fail to be truth-preserving in the positive semantics. That is, their appearing prima facie valid, noted at the beginning of this subsection, is misleading. Why is classical ∃-introduction invalid? Recall that, if c multiply signifies, then $\exists x(x = c)$ is evaluated false in every M^d-w.r.t.-M^R (so it is superfalse). However, $t = t$ is always true in every M^d-w.r.t.-M^R, no matter what t is. Either both sides of the identity statement are not ambiguous terms, in which case the formula is true before constructing complete disambiguations (i.e., the formula is true in the restricted model M^R), or both sides of the identity statement are ambiguous, in which case the formula is true in all complete disambiguations – and this latter includes the case of 'Charley = Charley.' But now we have a counterexample to ∃-introduction: $c = c$ is true, but $\exists x(x = c)$ is false. Since ∃-introduction is invalid for supervaluational consequence in a language with identity, it is also invalid for semi-classical consequence.

Why is classical ∀-introduction invalid in uniqueness-free languages containing identity, on the positive semantics? Since $t = t$ is always true in every M^d-w.r.t.-M^R, it follows that $t \neq t$ is always false, including the case where t is an ambiguous name. Now, since (to repeat) nothing in the domain is identical to Charley, the open formula $x \neq c$ is satisfied by every member of the domain. Thus, $\forall x(x \neq c)$ is true in M^R, and therefore true in every M^d-w.r.t.-M^R, while $c \neq c$ is false in every M^d-w.r.t.-M^R. That is, classical ∀-elimination is not sound in a language containing '=' (again, for both supervaluational and semi-classical consequence).

What changes should we make to the ∀-elimination and ∃-introduction rules, in order to make them valid in a multiply signifying language with identity?

One initially plausible idea is to try the same changes that existentially free logics make to ∀-elimination and ∃-introduction, which we saw in Section 4.2.1. As we saw there, existentially free logics introduce a monadic predicate $E!(x)$, whose intuitive meaning is 'x exists,' either as a new primitive predicate, or (in languages with identity) by definition as $\exists y(y = x)$. Then, they replace classical ∀-elimination with $\{\forall x F(x), E!(a)\} \vdash F(a)$, and replace classical ∃-introduction with $\{F(a), E!(a)\} \vdash \exists x F(x)$. That is, the existentially free rules simply add $E!(a)$ as a premise to each of the classical rules.

These changes do not work for uniqueness-free languages with the positive semantics. Why? First, suppose $E!$ has the meaning it does in existentially free logics. Then we cannot prove 'There is a big ant' from 'Charley is a big ant,' since we would lack the 'Charley exists' premise: $\exists x(x = c)$ is false. But one of the leading motivations for the supervaluational positive semantics was to legitimate this inference. Alternatively, we could say 'b exists' is true iff b has *at least one* referent (instead of exactly one referent). That is, replace $E!(a)$ in the above two existentially free proof rules with $E(a)$ (see p. 31) instead. This avoids the earlier problem: From 'Charley is a big ant' and 'Charley exists,' we could then derive 'There is a big ant' via the revised ∃-introduction rule. However, this solution generates a new problem. This revised ∃-introduction rule, which replaces $E!(a)$ with $E(a)$, would allow us to prove the false 'Something is identical to Charley' ($\exists x(x = c)$) from the two true claims 'Charley = Charley' and 'Charley exists.' (An analogous problem would affect an analogously-revised version of ∀-elimination.) We conclude this section with an open question: In (supervaluational and/or semi-classical) positive uniqueness-free logics with an interpreted identity predicate, are there reasonable proof rules for identity and the quantifiers that let us prove 'There is a big ant' from the conjunction of 'Charley exists' and 'Charley is a big ant,' without also letting us prove 'There is something identical to Charley'?

Languages without identity: Classical rules are sound. In the previous section, all the sentences that created problems involved identity. So one might wonder if all the problems might disappear if the language dropped '='. The answer is *yes*. Interestingly, the *classical* rules of ∀-elimination and ∃-introduction are sound in a uniqueness-free language, using the semi-classical or supervaluational notions of consequence, so long as the language does not contain an interpreted identity predicate. The proof for ∀-elimination can be found in Appendix 2.

Table 3 summarizes the last two subsections, stating the conditions under which classical ∀-elim and ∃-intro rules are sound in uniqueness-free languages for semi-classical and supervaluational consequence.

Table 3 Classical ∀-elim and ∃-intro in uniqueness-free logics

		Positive	**Neutral**	**Negative**
∀-elim	*without =*	FTP BFP	not FTP	not FTP
	with =	not FTP not BFP	BFP	not BFP
∃-intro	*without =*	FTP BFP	FTP	not FTP*
	with =	not FTP not BFP	not BFP	not BFP

Note: FTP: forward-truth preserving; BFP: backwards-falsehood preserving.
Note: * unless the sentence in the premise is atomic.

4.3.3 Positive Consequence: Subvaluational Semantics

The other positive semantics for uniqueness-free language (considered in Section 3.4.3) allowed a single ambiguous sentence to be both true and false at the same time, when that sentence is true on one disambiguation and false on another. This was called the 'subvaluational semantics.' Where the supervaluational semantics assigns a truth-value gap, the subvaluational semantics assigns a truth-value glut. (The converse does not hold: 'Ant A = Charley' is both true and false in the subvaluational semantics, but false in the supervaluational semantics, since it is assigned the value *false* (only) in the base restricted model.)

Because this semantics allows for sentences that are both true and false, any logical system using this semantics differs from other uniqueness-free systems. It is naturally captured by a paraconsistent logic of some sort.[56] A paraconsistent logic is one in which the classical principle 'Anything logically follows from a contradiction' is invalid. In classical logic (and other non-paraconsistent logics), a contradiction $A \land \neg A$ is necessarily false. So the argument $A \land \neg A$, *thus B* qualifies as valid in most logics, since it is impossible for the premise to be true and the conclusion untrue (since it is impossible for the premise to be true). However, if we allow sentences to be both true and false, as the Lewis-Priest subvaluational semantics does, then when A is both true and false, $A \land \neg A$ is also both true and false.[57] But then the argument $A \land \neg A$, *thus B* will be *invalid*, since there is a case where A is true (and false), and B is false only. There

---

[56] For an overview of paraconsistent logics, see Priest, Tanaka, & Weber (2022).

[57] The negation of a true and false sentence is, so to speak, false and true; a conjunction is true just in case both conjuncts are true, and is false iff at least one conjunct is false.

are many species of paraconsistent logics; Lewis proposes R-Mingle to handle ambiguity,[58] and Priest suggests his Logic of Paradox (LP).

Another important difference between these paraconsistent uniqueness-free logics and the others we have previously considered is that the =-elimination rule (p. 65), which holds in all the other existentially and uniqueness-free logics, does not hold in subvaluational semantics. In particular, transitivity of identity ($a = b$, $b = c$, *thus* $a = c$) is no longer truth-preserving. For on a subvaluational semantics, 'Ant A = Charley' and 'Charley = Ant B' will both be true (and false), but 'Ant A = Ant B' will be false only.

Recall from page 50 that Christina McLeish's semantics declares a sentence true if it is true on at least one disambiguation (like Lewis and Priest), but unlike Lewis and Priest, a sentence must be false on all disambiguations to count as false. Her system does not permit mixed disambiguations. As a result, on her semantics, ∧-intro is not sound. For example, suppose Ant A is eating, but Ant B is not. 'Charley is eating' will be true in the McLeish semantics (because of the Ant-A disambiguation), as will 'Charley is not eating' (because of the Ant-B disambiguation). But 'Charley is eating and Charley is not eating' will be false, since there is no disambiguation in which that conjunction is true.

For the propositional part of the language, Priest (1995, p. 365) claims that it is a proper sublogic of his Logic of Paradox (LP), without stating an explicitly exhaustive list of changes that need to be made to LP to arrive at a logic for ambiguous terms. It is proper because, in addition to transitivity of identity failing, ∃-Intro also fails, though not for the reason we have seen in the other generally free logics: In the subvaluational semantics, $\exists x(x = c)$ is true. But as we saw in the preceding paragraph, the Lewis-Priest semantics allows for mixed disambiguations, so 'Charley ≠ Charley' is both true and false (since 'Ant A ≠ Ant B' is true, and 'Ant A ≠ Ant A' is false). But $\exists x(x \neq x)$ is not true, so ∃-Intro fails. Lewis (1982, p. 439) claims that the purely propositional portion of a uniqueness-free language would be captured by the first-degree fragment of the relevance logic R-Mingle (RM),[59] if you wanted the proof rules to preserve truth in *all* (mixed) disambiguations, as opposed to preserving truth in at least one disambiguation.

There are other complications involved with these logical systems, just at the propositional level. For example, if we take the conditional $A \rightarrow B$ to be the standard material conditional $\neg A \vee B$, then the rule of modus ponens ($\{A, A \rightarrow B\}$, therefore B) is not valid in LP. However, other conditionals can be

---

[58] This logic results from adding the 'Mingle' axiom ($A \rightarrow (A \rightarrow A)$) to the relevance logic R (Mares, 2020). An overview of RM can be found in Dunn & Restall (2002, §3.10).

[59] Dunn (2021) is a general defense of RM for people who feel the appeal of relevance logic.

defined that validate modus ponens, though they each have their own idiosyn-crasies (Hazen & Pelletier, 2019). Interestingly, a leading candidate for such a conditional, if added to LP, would result in a logic perfectly translatable to the logic RM3,[60] the three-valued version of Lewis' preferred logic R-Mingle, which Lewis endorses as the right logic for ambiguity (Hazen & Pelletier, 2019, propositions 4 and 5).

5 Costs and Benefits of Each System

In Sections 3–4, we saw a wide array of logical systems designed to deal with words that are not univocal. Many people's interests lie less in the technical details of the logics themselves, and more in the philosophical applications of these logics to metaphysics, philosophy of language, and other areas outside of logic proper. Such readers might simply want to know: Which free logic is the correct one? Or at least the best one?

Unfortunately, such readers will be disappointed. In my opinion, no free logic is clearly superior to all the others. Each one has its own strengths and weak-nesses, but I do not see a principled, party-neutral way to determine whether a particular weakness is a deal-breaker, or instead that logic's strengths are pow-erful enough to overcome that weakness. For example, just how bad is it (if at all) if a position declares 'Zeus = Zeus' false? I believe reasonable people can disagree about this.

However, for readers who want to figure out which logic is best, given their own commitments, purposes, and values, this chapter is a tool to help them think through the main strengths and weaknesses of each logic – leaving it up to the reader to decide how bad each of the problems are, or how good each of the advantages are. Every position we've considered in this book involves picking some (apparent) poison, i.e. biting some (apparent) bullets. This chapter is a menu designed to help you pick your poison. Less metaphorically, you can understand which argumentative burdens you will have to assume, if you adopt a particular free logic.

The strengths and weaknesses are often comparative. So although the remainder of this section is organized into sections on neutral, negative, and positive free logics, each section mentions the other, competing types of logic. Finally, parts of this section may feel repetitive, since summarizing the pros and cons of each species of free logic requires us to look at the various traits of each species – traits which were presented in earlier sections.

---

[60] Tedder (2015) calls the resulting logic "A_3", in honor of Arnon Avron.

5.1 Neutral Free Logics

Pros. The central strength of a neutral semantics, as Lehmann (1994) explains, is that it honors an intuitive idea that forms the basis of much semantic theorizing: The semantic value of a sentence is a function of the semantic values of its parts. So if a string of linguistic characters needs semantic parts X, Y, and Z to have a truth-value, and one of those three parts is missing or otherwise defective, then the whole sentence's truth-value will also be missing or defective. Defective inputs lead to defective outputs. If you ask a graphing calculator to evaluate the function $f(x) = \frac{1}{x}$ at $x = 0$, you get an 'Error' message. And the second intuitive idea is that, for many sentences containing a name, to determine the truth-value of that sentence, you need the individual the name refers to as one of the inputs. From a semantic (but not grammatical) point of view, 'Pegasus is sleeping' and 'Charley is sleeping' are equivalent to '_____ is sleeping.' (Or the second might be '$\frac{\text{Ant A}}{\text{Ant B}}$ is sleeping,' but that is still clearly semantically defective: You cannot simultaneously cram two different inputs into a single one-place function.) For anyone committed to those two ideas, a neutral free logic is the most straightforward position.

A neutral free logic is not forced on you by those two commitments, but keeping them both without accepting a neutral free logic requires some contortions or extra burdens. For example, the second idea can be saved for empty names by positing an 'outer domain' which contains individuals that can be the referents of names like 'Vulcan,' but do not exist. While this is technically possible, many people will feel that the more natural position is that, for something to be an input (to any function), it must exist. And the negative semantics denies the first idea: On that semantics, defective inputs can lead to normal, non-defective outputs.

Cons. One key apparent problem with neutral free logics is that the set of logical truths shrinks significantly. How much it shrinks depends on whether one adopts the Weak Kleene or Strong Kleene scheme for $\wedge$ and $\vee$, and whether one accepts internal or external negation. Combining the Strong Kleene scheme with external negation will deliver several of the classical logical truths. For example, $A \vee \neg A$ will be true even when A has no truth-value, since $\neg A$ will be true (because negation is external), and any disjunction with at least one true disjunct is true (because we are using the Strong Kleene disjunction). If we use either Weak Kleene or internal negation, then $A \vee \neg A$ is not a logical truth. And thus (given the standard equivalence of $B \rightarrow C$ with $\neg B \vee C$), $A \rightarrow A$ is not a logical truth either. Existentially free neutral logic at least keeps logical truths that do not contain names, such as $\forall x(F(x) \rightarrow F(x))$. But in uniqueness-free logics, we even lose those too, since predicates like F can be undefined in uniqueness-free logics, though not in existentially free logics. But even in uniqueness-free logics, some logical truths remain, if the logic is first-order instead of propositional; for example, $\forall x(x = x)$ is true in all restricted models.

One natural reaction to this situation is to say that, in light of the considerations in the immediately preceding paragraph, the proponent of neutral logic should adopt the Strong Kleene scheme with external negation. From a technical point of view, this is certainly a possibility. However, it undermines the original motivation driving the neutral logic in the first place. Applying the 'Defective input, defective output' principle to compound sentences in propositional logic would support the Weak Kleene scheme and internal negation (Lehmann, 1994, p. 326). (The inputs are the truth-values of the component sentence(s), and the output is the truth-value of the resulting compound sentence.)

Alternatively, one might attempt to lessen the sting of a neutral free logic shrinking the number of logical truths in a couple of ways. To begin with, one might claim that it is not very important, for two reasons. First, although these classical logical truths are not logical *truths* in neutral free logic, nonetheless they are never false. And perhaps a guarantee of non-falsity is good enough. Lehmann (1994, p. 314) suggestively calls such sentences "weakly logically true." At least, this looks better than saying certain sentences of the form $b = b$ are *false*, as the negative free logician does (and the Lewis-Priest positive logic says some sentences of the form $b = b$ are both true and false). Second, although neutral free logic 'loses' many classical logical *truths*, it still classifies many classically valid *arguments* as truth-preserving. As we just saw, the sentence $A \rightarrow A$ is not a logical truth, but the argument A, *thus A* is still truth-preserving.[61] The same holds for a number of other classical logical truths that are not logical truths in a neutral logic. For example, *modus ponens* is still truth-preserving, even though its sentence analog $((A \rightarrow B) \wedge A) \rightarrow B$ is not a logical truth. And perhaps losing the logical truths is not so bad, as long as we can keep logically correct arguments. This line of thought leads us to a difficult question, which we will not pursue here: What is the use or value of logical truths, over and above valid arguments? The other general way to respond to neutral logics' reduction in the number of logical truths is to say that this is actually a welcome conclusion, and is independently motivated for other reasons. Many philosophers, most famously Quine, have been skeptical of the existence of analytic truths, sentences true in virtue of their meaning alone. Logical

---

[61] Thus complete neutral logics do not obey the deduction theorem, namely: If there is a proof of C from $P_1, P_2, \ldots P_n$, then there is a proof of $(P_1 \wedge P_2 \wedge \ldots \wedge P_n) \rightarrow C$.

truths are paradigm examples of analytic truths, for both the friends and foes of analyticity. Even Quine allows that if there were any analytic truths, then the logical truths would be the clearest examples of them (Quine, 1960, p. 65). Thus, one straightforward way to deny the existence of analytic truths is to deny there are any logical truths. For example, Penelope Maddy (2007) makes the argument that naturalists skeptical of analytic truths should adopt a propositional logic based on the Weak Kleene scheme, including internal negation. J. C. Beall (2018) makes a related argument for the superiority of the relevant logic of First-Degree Entailment over classical logic, on the grounds that logic should be kept separate from theories (in the sense of claims): We want logic to leave possibilities open. So for some people, neutral free logics' lack of logical truths is a feature, not a bug.

5.2 Negative Free Logics

Pros. There are a number of interrelated reasons why one might want to adopt a negative semantics for languages containing defective names.[62] First, one might hold that what it means for a linguistic expression to be false just is to be an untrue declarative sentence. If you combine that with the view that simple sentences with defective names or predicates cannot be true, then negative free logic results. Second, one might be committed to bivalence, perhaps because one thinks it is simpler for every sentence to be true or false (and never both), and simplicity is a criterion for selecting a logic. This criterion does not distinguish negative free logic from the inner-domain/outer-domain positive semantics, which is also bivalent, but it does distinguish it from all the other positive and neutral options. (Also, the inner-domain/outer-domain semantics is only available for existentially free logics, not uniqueness-free ones; the negative semantics is the only uniqueness-free semantics on offer that preserves bivalence.)

Third, one might be favorably disposed, for independent reasons, toward classical logic, and thus want to retain as much of it as possible. In certain important ways, negative free logic is closer to classical logic than the other options. For example, the negative semantics uses exactly the classical truth-tables, taking them over without any alterations. This is a consequence of its being bivalent; thus the inner-domain/outer-domain semantics can also

---

[62] One relatively early defense is in Burge (1974). A more recent book-length elaboration of the view can be found in Sainsbury (2005), which has generated a number of commentaries and responses (see Orlando [2008] and Dumitru & Kroon [2008], among others). Also useful and important is Braun (1993). These are primarily works in the philosophy of language, as opposed to logic proper.

use the classical truth tables, though the other semantics cannot. And the inner-domain/outer-domain semantics conflicts with classical logic insofar as the extensions of names and predicates are not confined to the domain of quantification, unlike the negative semantics.

Cons.   However, negative free logic does conflict with classical logic in certain ways. And it does so in particularly counter-intuitive places (as opposed to, for example, rejecting the counter-intuitive classical theorem that every sentence follows from a contradiction, as paraconsistent logics do). Specifically, $b = b$ is not a logical truth, because 'Zeus = Zeus' and 'Charley = Charley' are both false.[63] And thus, perhaps even less intuitively, 'Zeus ≠ Zeus' and 'Charley ≠ Charley' are both true. For many people, this consequence of negative semantics is too high a price to pay for getting rid of truth-valueless sentences, and serves as a reductio ad absurdum of negative free logic.

That said, the negative free logicians can present the following counter-argument in favor of 'Pegasus = Pegasus' being false. Even the positive free logicians agree that '$\exists x(x = \text{Pegasus})$' should not come out as true. If that is right, then there should not be *any* name you could plug into the open formula '$x = \text{Pegasus}$' that would make it true.[64] But the positive free logicians hold that plugging the name 'Pegasus' in for x does result in a true sentence. So in short, the positive free logicians' own belief that '$\exists x(x = \text{Pegasus})$' is false should lead them to reject their belief that 'Pegasus = Pegasus' is true. Additionally, Sainsbury (2004), a proponent of negative free logic, suggests that we can draw a distinction between (i) 'It is not the case that Pegasus = Pegasus,' and (ii) 'Pegasus is non-identical with Pegasus.' If we further take 'is non-identical with Pegasus' as a simple predicate (despite its typical representation), then (ii) will be false on free logic, though (i) is still true. And the falsehood of (i) perhaps feels less objectionable than making (ii) false.[65]

---

[63]   Burge (1974, §IV) argues for the falsity of self-identities with empty names, like 'Zeus = Zeus.' Peacock and Tedder (2016) also offer an independent defense of this prima facie unintuitive consequence: They go even further than a proponent of negative free logic, denying that $\forall x(x = x)$ should be a theorem. Finally, some people have suggested that dropping the law of identity is one fruitful way to grasp some of the strange traits of quantum particles; the collection of essays in Arenhart & Arroyo (2023) provides the state of the art in this field.

[64]   One might suspect this argument tacitly assumes the heterodox 'substitutional' (as opposed to 'objectual') conception of quantification, since it talks about substituting a name for a variable. (For more on this distinction, see, e.g., MacFarlane [2021, §2.4]). However, it does not. This argument merely requires $\exists x\phi(x)$ be true if there is at least one name that can be plugged in for x in $\phi(x)$ to generate a true sentence. But this argument does *not* require the other, 'only if' direction, which is the more contentious part of substitutional quantification.

[65]   Thanks to an anonymous referee for making this connection to Sainsbury's work.

A second problem with negative free logic stems from the fact that atomic sentences are treated differently, logically speaking, from non-atomic sentences. Recall the Negative E!-Intro rule (p. 64): one may derive $E!(b)$ from $\phi(b)$, if $\phi(b)$ is atomic. But if $\phi(b)$ is not atomic, $E!(b)$ does not follow.[66] Considered in isolation, this fact about negative free logic may appear to be a mere technical curiosity rather than a strength or a weakness. However, it becomes a potential problem when one recognizes that there are sets of predicates that are logically interdefinable with one another, and thus which predicates are taken as primitive or basic, and which predicates are taken as defined, is a completely arbitrary choice. For example, any of the following three predicates are definable in terms of the other two: (i) 'smaller than,' (ii) 'same size as,' and (iii) 'bigger than.' We can define (iii) in terms of (i) and (ii) as follows:

x is bigger than $y =_{\text{def}} \neg(x$ smaller than $y) \wedge \neg(x$ is the same size as $y)$

Now consider the sentence 'Paris is smaller than Jakarta.' Using the E!-Intro rule, we can derive 'Paris exists' and 'Jakarta exists' from this sentence, assuming (as in the definition just above) 'smaller than' is a basic predicate. Note that 'Paris is smaller than Jakarta' is equivalent (given our definition) to 'Jakarta is bigger than Paris.' Now consider the 'defined' version of 'Jakarta is bigger than Paris,' namely:

$\neg$ (Jakarta is smaller than Paris) $\wedge \neg$ (Jakarta is the same size as Paris).

We cannot derive the sentences 'Paris exists' and 'Jakarta exists' from this sentence, despite the fact that this sentence is logically equivalent (given the definition) to the previous sentence 'Paris is smaller than Jakarta.' But logically equivalent sentences should have the same logical consequences. That seems bad enough, but matters are even worse: If we had instead defined 'smaller' in terms of 'same size' and 'bigger,' then 'Paris is smaller than Jakarta' – the first sentence we considered – would not entail 'Paris exists' or 'Jakarta exists.' So one and the same sentence can entail or not entail some conclusion, depending on the completely arbitrary and symmetric decision of which of (i)–(iii) we decide to define in terms of the other two. For more on this argument, see Nolt (2010, §4.1).

Here is a third and final possible problem with negative free logic. It is provable in negative free logic that all non-existents are indiscernable (Pavlović & Gratzl, 2021, p. 126); that is:

---

[66] This is also a property of neutral free logics, unless that neutral logic declares $E!(b)$ false for non-univocal b (in which case, this E!-Intro rule is forward truth-preserving but not backwards falsehood-preserving).

$$\neg E!(a) \wedge \neg E!(b) \vdash F(\ldots a \ldots) \rightarrow F(\ldots b \ldots) \qquad \text{(IndiscNon-Ex)}$$

Some people will reject the claim that Santa Claus shares all the same properties with Zeus. That said, proponents of negative existentially free logic would probably not be bothered about this fact about their preferred logic. They might even welcome it: After all, how could two non-entities differ from one another? There are not two different nothings, with different properties; the empty set is unique.[67] However, this reply is far less convincing in the case of uniqueness-free languages. It seems very implausible to say that Q (of QAnon) and Homer share all their properties. So even if this reply is acceptable for an existentially free logic, it seems less plausible for a uniqueness-free logic. The positive free description theory FD2, which we saw on page 44, is characterized by a principle that is similar to (IndiscNon-Ex), namely:

$$(\neg E!(t_1) \wedge \neg E!(t_2)) \rightarrow t_1 = t_2 \qquad \text{(FD2)}$$

for any two singular terms t_1, t_2, including definite descriptions. And FD2 is a positive theory. So the point about Q and Homer just above applies to this positive theory as well, since 'Q = Homer' should intuitively be untrue.

5.3 Positive Free Logics

This section is more complicated than the previous two, since we have discussed multiple, fairly different positive proposals: inner-domain/outer-domain semantics (for existentially free only), subvaluational semantics (for uniqueness-free only), and supervaluations (for both, but there are differences between existentially free and uniqueness-free cases). Thus, this subsection will also discuss in-fighting among the positive free logics, for example, whether ambiguity should be handled with supervaluations or with a subvaluational semantics.

Pros.   First, as has been mentioned multiple times already, all of the positive semantics make $b = b$ logically true, and $b \neq b$ logically false, unlike negative and neutral free logics. That said, in the Lewis-Priest logics, when b is an ambiguous name, $b = b$ will be both true *and* false, as will $b \neq b$. So, unintuitively, $b = b$ is 'no more true' than $b \neq b$, and $b \neq b$ is 'no more false' than $b = b$. Thus, although $b = b$ is a logical truth in the Lewis-Priest semantics, it

---

[67] This reply is why a particular old Soviet-era joke is funny. A man goes into a shop and asks, "You don't have any meat?" "No," replies the sales lady, "We don't have any fish. It's the store across the street that doesn't have any meat" (CIA, 2016). If the negative free logician's reply were wrong, and there really were two different kinds of nothing, then the shopkeeper's response would be completely normal, not funny.

is *not* a logical non-falsehood. And therefore it is not clear if the Lewis-Priest semantics is better than the neutral semantics, which is the mirror-image of this case: On the neutral semantics, $b = b$ is not logically true, but it is also logically not false.

Now, one might ask: Is it really that intuitive that 'Zeus = Zeus' and 'Charley = Charley' are true? The positive logicians report that they have an intuition that those sentences seem true to them.[68] But if it is merely their intuition, then the negative and (especially) neutral logicians can say that they have a different intuition, and there is no compelling reason to favor one group's intuitions over the other groups' intuitions.

This line of thought leads to a second consideration in favor of the positive semantics. The positive proposals fit survey data about naive informants' reactions to sentences containing empty or ambiguous names better than the neutral and negative semantics do. Piccinini and Scott (2010) asked study participants to make truth-value judgments about sentences containing vacuous names. The participants' replies matched the truth-value assignments of positive semantics far better than the other two semantics. For example, for the sentence 'Santa Claus is fat,' about 82% of respondents said it was true, 7% said it was false, 4% said it had no truth-value, and 7% chose 'Don't know / It depends.' (Interestingly, as names are further removed from ordinary, English-sounding words, participants' responses become closer to the truth-value assignments of neutral free logic. For example, about 58% of respondents said the 'sentence' 'sdfs-dfsdf does not exist' had no truth-value, whereas only 20% said that sentence is true.) The data Piccinini and Scott collected favors the inner-domain/outer-domain semantics over the supervaluational one, since on the supervaluational semantics, 'Santa Claus is fat' is neither true nor false.

Frost-Arnold and Beebe (2020) ran a similar study for ambiguous names. Their results were similar: Survey responses were highly correlated with the truth-values assigned by positive semantics. And just as in the existentially-free case, the competition between semantic proposals was not close. The sentence 'Charley is an ant' was considered true by about 82% of survey participants, false by 4%, and neither true nor false by 3% (10% said 'Both true and false,' and 1% said 'Don't know'). Interestingly, for some questions the subvaluational semantics provided better predictions than the supervaluational semantics (e.g., 'Charley is eating now,' when Ant A is eating but Ant B is not), and for other questions the situation was reversed (e.g., 'Charley = Charley').

---

[68] Bacon (2013, p. 6–8) provides a wide-ranging list of types of sentences containing empty names that intuitively seem to be true, even though the supervaluational semantics would classify them as neither true nor false.

The data collected in these two studies should not be taken as conclusive evidence that (at least one of) the positive semantics are right, and negative and neutral semantics are wrong. Naive informants' truth-value judgments do not definitively settle logical questions: Paradoxes demonstrate that our naive reactions are often inconsistent when taken together. Furthermore, naive informants' elicited responses about truth-values are often affected by pragmatic factors instead of semantic ones alone.[69] That said, a semantic theory of a language should not float free of language-users' truth-value judgments; the survey responses should serve as some constraint on semantic theorizing.

Restricting attention to languages with ambiguity, there is a third reason in favor of positive semantics: Positive uniqueness-free logics distinguish ambiguous names from empty ones, whereas negative and neutral semantics collapse that distinction. For although there are supervaluational semantics available for both ambiguous and empty names, those two semantics are somewhat different from each other, as we saw in Section 3.4.2. Using a negative or neutral semantics for ambiguous names in effect treats 'Zeus' and 'Charley' as logically the same kind of thing. Of course, both are cases of defective reference, and they are similar in that way. But the types of defect are different: Not enough reference is distinct from too much reference. The negative or neutral proponent might respond, perhaps by appealing to the goal of maximizing theoretical simplicity, that failures of univocal reference should be given uniform treatment. But that increased simplicity must be weighed against the fact that the negative and neutral options for ambiguous language throw away information contained in M^U that the positive semantics preserve. Consider a mathematical analogy: Both '$\frac{1}{0}$' and '$\sqrt{9}$' fail to refer univocally. But it seems reasonable to say, for example, that the absolute value of $\sqrt{9}$ is less than 5, and that $\sqrt{9}^2 = 9$. But we cannot say anything similarly specific about the absolute value of $\frac{1}{0}$, or its square. On this analogy, the negative and neutral semantics treat '$\frac{1}{0}$' and '$\sqrt{9}$' the same, while the positive semantics does not. Similarly, compare the question 'Superman, where are you now?' to 'Charley,

---

[69] See von Fintel (2004). Here is an example where an informant might say that a false sentence is true, because of pragmatic factors. Suppose our mutual friend, who is known to be overly enthusiastic about Apple products, is coming over to visit me today. Looking out the window, I see him walking up to my door, and say to you: 'Steve Jobs is almost here.' If I asked naive informants whether this sentence is true, many would respond that it is, even though its content is literally, i.e., semantically, false (assuming the ghost of Steve Jobs does not appear in my home in the next few minutes). Such informants are responding to the fact that I communicated something true via Gricean conversational implicature, which is part of pragmatics, not semantics. In Kripkean terms, the "speaker's reference" of my utterance of 'Steve Jobs' is our mutual friend, while the "semantic reference" of that utterance is the cofounder of Apple who died in 2011 (Kripke, 1977).

where are you now?' One might reasonably say that Charley is located in Fred's ant colony – but Superman is nowhere (actual – i.e., nowhere non-fictional). Although the neutral and negative semantics have the advantage of being simpler than the positive semantics, they suffer from the disadvantage of throwing away information.

Cons. One aspect of positive semantics for empty names that many people find worrying is its need for some sort of non-existent entities. Some people consider the inner-domain/outer-domain semantics philosophically suspect, on the grounds that the elements of the outer domain seem to be ontologically extravagant, or otherwise metaphysically mysterious.[70] Although this 'spooky metaphysics' concern obviously applies to the inner-domain/outer-domain semantics, it also applies (arguably to a lesser extent) to the supervaluational semantics for empty names (Bacon, 2013, p. 9). Recall from Section 3.4.2, p. 46 that, to prevent $\forall x F(x) \vdash F(a)$ and $F(a) \vdash \exists x F(x)$ from being supervaluationally valid, we had to allow completion models whose domains include elements that are not in the 'base' model's domain (this difference being captured formally by $D \subset D^c$). A supervaluationist might argue that there is an important ontological difference between the members of the outer domain and the members of $D^c - D$,[71] but they seem very similar, at least on their face. So, if you find the prospect of semantic theorizing in terms of non-existing entities unappealing, then positive free logic is probably not for you.[72]

Setting that concern aside, suppose one wanted to accept positive free logic for empty names. Which semantics is superior? The main advantage the supervaluationist claims over the inner-domain/outer-domain semantics is that the supervaluationist need not be committed to the truth or falsity of claims about entities in the outer domain that do not appear to be determinate. The sentences that seem like they should be truth-valueless *are* truth-valueless, on a

---

[70] For example, Restall (2006, p. 202); Bencivenga says this view is common, and adds "apparently researchers held back from pursuing or publishing completeness results utilizing alternative approaches [including inner-domain/outer-domain semantics] because of philosophical worries about their significance" (Bencivenga, 1990, p. 15). However, some have argued that the outer domain is philosophically innocuous, and does not require Meinongianism (Lambert & van Fraassen, 1972, p. 200).

[71] Bencivenga (2002, p. 177) makes this argument: "[I]n outer domain semantics non-denoting singular terms simply 'denote' non-existents, whereas in [Bencivenga's preferred supervaluational] approach these terms denote nothing, and we only take the liberty of considering *alternative* situations (or 'possible worlds') where they denote, and of making their behavior there relevant for the evaluation of sentences containing them in the situations (or worlds) where they do not denote."

[72] Bacon (2013) offers a proposal for how to escape this apparent problem; a central move is to use a free metatheory, thereby allowing some properties to be existence-entailing and others not.

supervaluationist approach. There does not appear to be anything that could determine whether Pegasus falls under the extension of 'weighs less than 700 kilograms' or not. Is the number of hairs on Santa Claus's head odd or even? There does not seem to be anything (non-arbitrary) that could answer that question.[73] The supervaluationist points out that their position eliminates this arbitrariness by assigning truth-values according to *all* possible arbitrary ways of filling in the stories of Pegasus and Santa.

But the inner-domain/outer-domain proponent can lodge reasonable complaints against the supervaluationist as well. The inner-domain/outer-domain semantics restores bivalence to the language. Additionally, from a more technical point of view, inner-domain/outer-domain semantics is strongly complete and can be axiomatized, unlike supervaluational consequence (p. 68). Finally, the only way to prevent supervaluationism from violating core commitments of free logic (e.g., $\forall x F(x) \rightarrow F(a)$ is not a logical truth) is ad hoc, since it introduces the complication of 'truth in M^c-w.r.t.-M^R' without any independent motivation, other than preventing the supervaluationist proposal from being refuted. (Obviously, if you find all of the objections in the last three paragraphs compelling, then you should adopt a neutral or negative semantics for empty names.)

This final concern, about the ad hoc nature of how supervaluations avoid refutation by adding complexities, applies also to using supervaluations to deal with ambiguity. (However, there is no need for non-existent entities in the domain, unlike supervaluations in existentially free logics.) The cumbersome 'M^c-w.r.t.-M^R' apparatus was introduced precisely because the apparently false 'There is exactly one Charley' is true in every disambiguation, and that unwelcome consequence of a simple, straightforward supervaluationism had to be blocked somehow.

For the subvaluational positive logics of Lewis and Priest, it is perhaps more difficult to create a list of uncontroversial prima facie potential costs. That is because what many people will consider disadvantages of these logics will be considered advantages (or at least neutral or conducive of advantages) by others. Specifically, many people are hesitant to say that some sentences can be both true and false at the same time. However, proponents of paraconsistent logic typically arrived at their view independently of concerns about ambiguity. Paraconsistent logicians are often motivated first and foremost by the desire to invalidate the (unintuitive) classical principle that anything logically follows from a contradiction ($A \wedge \neg A$, thus B), and to do that (while maintaining that validity is a matter of truth-preservation), there needs to

---

[73] Berto (2013, §5.3.3) calls this the 'Problem of Additional Properties' for Meinongianism.

be a true contradiction. So treating some ambiguous sentences as both true and false actually bolsters paraconsistent logicians' antecedently preferred, independently motivated view.

On the other hand, if one is not already positively disposed toward paraconsistency, perhaps the intuitive strangeness of true contradictions can be lessened by holding (with Lewis) that no *propositions* need be both true and false on the subvaluational semantics. Instead, only *sentences* need be both true and false: A sentence can be ambiguous between a true proposition and a false proposition. For a final reason to prefer the Lewis-Priest semantics over the supervaluational ones, Priest claims that "truth-values of sentences with multiple denotations are, in a very clear sense, overdetermined, not underdetermined" (Priest, 1995, p. 368). As evidence for Priest's claim, this would explain why the everyday answer to an ambiguous question is typically 'Yes and no,' not 'Neither yes nor no.'

Note that all the points in the previous paragraph generally favor the existence of some sentences that are both true and false. One might find that general idea plausible, yet still disagree with some of the particular truth-value assignments of the subvaluational semantics. For example, one might think that 'Charley = Charley' should not be classified as false (even if it is also classified as true), or that 'There is exactly one thing identical to Charley' should not be classified as true (even if it is also classified as false). So while someone who finds the independent arguments for paraconsistent logics plausible might be inclined toward the Lewis-Priest semantics, that alone does not settle the matter in favor of the Lewis-Priest semantics.

6 Conclusion: Revisiting the Motivations

We have now seen some of what happens logically, both from the point of view of semantics and of proofs, when we relax the assumption that names and predicates refer uniquely. Semantically, this results in switching from classical logic's (total) interpretation function to an interpretation relation where names and predicates are also allowed to be semantically related to nothing in the domain of the model. Proof-theoretically, this results in the classical rules for ∀-Elimination and ∃-Introduction (almost always) being weakened. The exact form of the weakening varies from one free logic to another, with the limiting case being uniqueness-free logics without identity on a semi-classical conception of consequence, where those two classical rules are still valid.

This Element aims not only to describe free logics for their own sake, but also to highlight some of their applications to other areas of philosophy. So let us briefly return in this conclusion to the applications of free logics outlined in Section 2, armed with more knowledge now.

As we saw in Section 2.3.2, free logics are intertwined with the scientific realism versus anti-realism debates. Failures of univocality are one kind of mismatch between our language and our world. One concern was that failures of univocality might push us into *semantic* anti-realism about theoretical scientific discourse, the view that portions of scientific theories are neither true nor false. But this is a view that many current philosophers, both realists and anti-realists, want to avoid. With Sections 3–5 under our belts, we can imagine a number of ways to avoid semantic anti-realism. First, negative free logics are an available option, and they completely eliminate all truth-value gaps, unlike the neutral and supervaluational semantics. Second, instead of thinking that ambiguous terms lead to truth-value gaps, one might hold instead that they lead to truth-value *gluts*. In the case of scientific vocabulary, too much reference (ambiguity) is arguably more common than too little reference (empty names), because much superseded scientific vocabulary should perhaps not be thought of as referring to nothing whatsoever, but rather as having an ambiguous or confused connection to the world. For example, when Joseph Priestley thought of phlogiston as something like the material stuff emitted in combustion, he was *not* thinking of absolutely nothing. The stuff that is emitted in combustion (primarily CO_2) is not the same as what it is in substances that makes them flammable, even though Priestley conceived of phlogiston in both of those two ways.

For some people, shifting from truth-value gaps to truth-value gluts is jumping out of the frying pan and into the fire: This move saves us from the letter of semantic anti-realism, but at the cost of being saddled with dialetheism, which many people will consider an even worse consequence. That said, recall that the form of dialethia proposed here is at the level of *sentences*, not the more controversial level of a proposition being both true and false simultaneously.[74]

Additionally, thinking of claims couched in superseded ambiguous language as generating truth-value gluts complicates how to conceptualize the realism debate itself, which is typically framed as the question of whether we have good reason to think that scientific theories are true or not. It is not clear whether going subvaluationist should count as a realist view, or an anti-realist view. People sometimes suggest that the realism debate is something to be dissolved instead of solved in favor of one party or the other; subvaluationism might be

---

[74] There is already an established philosophical area studying 'inconsistent science' (Vickers, 2013), but that typically examines inconsistencies within a given science, or between contemporaneously accepted sciences, and thus inconsistency at the level of propositions. Also, this literature is not directly relevant to the comparison between our current scientific language and bygone, superseded scientific language.

one way to dissolve the question, or declare a 'tie' (or something like it). Finally, admitting truth-value gluts might even provide some help for the perennially tricky notion, central to the realism debates, of 'approximate truth': Perhaps we could take an ambiguous sentence to be approximately true, if it is true on most of its disambiguations, and approximately false if it is false on most of its disambiguations.

What about the problem of empty names, and the other problems in language and metaphysics described in Section 2.3.1? Supervaluational approaches were intended to deliver us from some of the more counterintuitive consequences of negative and neutral free logics, without falling into something like Meinongianism. In my estimation, we have seen that the prospects for this are not as good as one might have hoped, because for supervaluations to deliver the 'right' results (i.e., to avoid validating ∀-Elimination and ∃-Introduction), they have to include elements in the domain of the completion models that are not elements of the domain of the base model. And these 'extra' elements of the completion models seem very similar to the elements of the outer domain. One might have wanted to avoid positing something like a Meinongian realm, and also maintain that $b = b$ is a logical truth, but those two options do not allow for that possibility. Antonelli's semantics does allow for both of those, but as things currently stand, the technical apparatus that accomplishes that is not very well motivated. Perhaps his formalism can be given a plausible and motivated interpretation in the future; that would be a welcome advance.

Can the contents of this Element shed any light on the apparent problems raised by slow-switch thought experiments? In a slow-switch case, someone is abducted without their knowledge from our Earth and taken to Twin Earth. Then, after being on Twin Earth for many years, they make the following inference:

(P1) When I was a child, my mother's favorite necklace was made of gold.
(P2) My current favorite ring is made of gold.
   Thus, my current favorite ring, and my mother's favorite necklace when I was a child, are both gold.

The problems arose from the natural thought that 'gold' in P1 means Earth-gold, and the 'gold' in P2 means Twin-gold. To preserve our ability to tell whether two of our beliefs are the same or different, and to keep logic a priori, Recanati in effect adopts a neutral semantics for ambiguous terms. Specifically, he holds that the inter-world traveler's confusion entails that the word 'gold' fails to refer to anything, and any thoughts involving such confused words and concepts are truth-valueless.

How can what we have seen in previous sections help in evaluating Recanati's view? First, moving from classical logic to a neutral free logic does save the a priori status of logic. However, as we saw in Section 5.1, a neutral semantics leads to very few or no sentences being propositional logical truths (depending on whether we adopt the Weak or Strong Kleene scheme, and internal or external negation). So this way of saving the a priori status of logic is arguably a Pyrrhic victory: All the logical truths are known a priori, but this is vacuously (or almost vacuously) true, since there are no (or almost no) logical truths. Second, Recanati's position has been criticized on the grounds that the traveler rehearsing P1 and P2 above seems to be having some sort of thoughts (Coliva & Belleri, 2013, p. 112); contra Recanati, the traveler does not seem to be thinking nothing, even if what they are thinking is not perfectly clear and unambiguous.

We can keep Recanati's core proposal that every instance of 'gold' is confused, and address both of these concerns, by replacing Recanati's neutral semantics with a supervaluational semantics instead. The classical propositional logical truths would then be restored, and the traveler's thoughts have some content (even though that content is not univocal: The traveler is thinking two thoughts, instead of none). Additionally, if we recall the topic of teleosemantic indeterminacy, adopting a supervaluational semantics there would also provide a regimented and precise way to talk about a cognitive state that represents multiple contents simultaneously, an idea which Bergman (2023) leaves at an intuitive level.

Finally, there is more work left to be done on free logics, and especially on uniqueness-free logics, which have been studied far less than existentially free logics. In particular, definite descriptions, which have been the subject of extensive research in existentially free logics, lack a sustained treatment in uniqueness-free logics. And one thing that readers might have been expecting in this Element that does not appear is a fully combined treatment of a language containing both empty names and ambiguity. Only a relatively small amount of that work has been presented here. The primary reason is that, as we have seen, there is a wide variety of available logical proposals for dealing with both types of non-univocal terms, so the number of possible combinations is quite high. Also, since uniqueness-free languages have been far less studied than existentially free ones, I thought it better to describe them here in isolation, to more clearly discern their similarities and differences from traditional, existentially free logics. But a very interesting area for future research involves how best to combine the two different kinds of failures of univocality into a single, philosophically and logically coherent account.

Appendix 1
Anti-satisfaction for Compound Expressions

In the classical case, a formula is true if every sequence satisfies it, and false if no sequence satisfies it. This creates problems when we want to allow for sentences that have an undefined truth-value: No sequence will satisfy a formula with undefined terms or predicate letters. Therefore, if we used the classical rules, formulas that we want to model as lacking truth-values would all be assigned the truth-value *false*. That is, in classical contexts, a sequence either satisfies a formula or it does not. However, in the cases of interest here, we need to leave open the possibility that a sequence could do neither. We do this by introducing 'satisfaction'/'anti-satisfaction' (analogous to 'extension'/'anti-extension' for predicates).

First, we slightly modify the notion of a valuation (or evaluation). Let t be an individual constant or a variable. Given a restricted model $M^R(= \langle D, f^R \rangle)$, let Σ be the set of all denumerable sequences of D. For each sequence $s = (s_1, s_2, \ldots) \in \Sigma$, we define a function v^* (often called a *valuation* or evaluation) that takes terms in L to elements of D, as follows:

- If t is a variable x_i, then $v^*(t)$ is s_i.
- If t is an individual constant a_i, then $v^*(t) = f^R(a_i)$; if $f^R(a_i)$ is undefined, so is $v^*(t)$. (This final clause is the only change to the usual notion of a valuation.)

We also say that a wff ϕ is *defined* on a model M iff that model's interpretation function assigns values to all (individual, predicate, and function) constants in ϕ.

For atomic formulae defined on M^R, the conditions for satisfaction are just the standard ones familiar from Tarski onwards. For atomic formulas not defined on M^R, however, things are not so simple. For unlike the classical case, there are two ways in which a sequence can fail to satisfy a formula, analogous to the difference between truth-valueless sentences and false sentences: Either the formula is not sufficiently semantically defined, or the formula is semantically defined but the sequence does not satisfy it. We will call the latter 'anti-satisfaction.'

A sequence s *anti-satisfies* an atomic formula ϕ in M if either:

- ϕ is defined on M, and s does not satisfy ϕ in M, or
- ϕ is an atomic formula of the form $t_1 = t_2$, and exactly one of $v^*(t_1)$ and $v^*(t_2)$ is undefined.[1]

---

[1] This modification has been used for decades in existentially free logics; see Lambert (2001, p. 267–270).

As a result of this second condition, the open formulas 'x = Charley' and 'x = Zeus' are anti-satisfied by every sequence, since variables count as defined.

For compound expressions, we cannot carry over the usual definition of satisfaction for compound expressions unaltered, if the definition relies on the notion of 's does not satisfy ϕ.' For example, in the classical case, a sequence s satisfies $\neg\phi$ iff s does not satisfy ϕ. But if we want our negation to follow the truth-table for 'weak/internal' negation, this classical satisfaction rule delivers the wrong result, since it will declare certain sentences false that should be truth-valueless instead. Thus, we modify the satisfaction condition for internal/weak negation to use the notion of anti-satisfaction instead, as follows:

- s satisfies $\neg\phi$ iff
  - s anti-satisfies ϕ.   (internal/weak negation)
  - s does not satisfy ϕ.   (external/strong negation)

Disjunctions also require a similar alteration in the definition of satisfaction under the Weak Kleene scheme (the Strong Kleene disjunction just uses the classical definition).

- s satisfies $\phi \vee \psi$ iff
  - ϕ and ψ are defined, and s satisfies at least one of ϕ, ψ.   (Weak Kleene)
  - s satisfies at least one of ϕ, ψ.   (Strong Kleene)

These two pairs of definitions would give us four different definitions of satisfaction for conditional statements, if one accepts the equivalence of $A \rightarrow B$ with $\neg A \vee B$.

The anti-satisfaction conditions for compound expressions can be formulated in a straightforward way:

- s anti-satisfies $\neg\phi$ iff
  - ϕ is defined and s does not satisfy ϕ.   (internal negation)
  - s does not satisfy ϕ.   (external negation)
- s anti-satisfies $\phi \vee \psi$ iff s anti-satisfies ϕ and s anti-satisfies ψ.
- s anti-satisfies $\phi \wedge \psi$ iff
  - ϕ and ψ are defined, and s anti-satisfies at least one of ϕ, ψ.

                                   (Weak Kleene)
  - s anti-satisfies at least one of ϕ, ψ.   (Strong Kleene)
- s anti-satisfies $\exists x_i \phi$ iff every sequence that differs from s in at most the ith place anti-satisfies ϕ.

Appendix 2

Soundness of Classical ∀-Elim for Uniqueness-Free Semantics without '='

I claimed in Section 4.3.2 that the *classical* rules of ∀-elimination and ∃-introduction are sound in a uniqueness-free language, using the semi-classical or supervaluational notions of consequence, so long as the language does not contain an interpreted identity predicate. Let us see why, for the case of ∀-elimination. Since every semi-classically valid argument is supervaluationally valid (as we saw in Section 4.3.2), we will only discuss the semi-classical case. We need to show that if $\forall x \phi(x)$ is true in an arbitrary M^d-w.r.t.-M^R, then $\phi(b)$ is also true in that same M^d-w.r.t.-M^R, even when ϕ and/or b are ambiguous. Now, there are two ways for $\forall x \phi(x)$ to be true in M^d-w.r.t.-M^R: either it is true already in M^R (in which case its truth-value in any M^d is irrelevant to its truth-value in M^d-w.r.t-M^R), or it is truth-valueless in M^R but true in M^d. Let us consider these two cases separately.

Case 1. If $\forall x \phi(x)$ is true in the 'base' model M^R, then every symbol in ϕ is defined in M^R. (Note: This would not be the case if our language contained '=': $\forall x (x \neq c)$ is true in M^R, when c is ambiguous.) If b is also defined in M^R, then of course $\phi(b)$ will be true in M^R (and thus M^d-w.r.t.-M^R) too, since everything is completely classical. So consider the case where b is ambiguous. If every symbol in ϕ is defined in M^R, and (as we assumed) $\forall x \phi(x)$ is true in M^R, then it will also be true in every disambiguation model M^d. So in each disambiguation model, every individual in that model's domain will satisfy $\phi(x)$. Therefore, no matter which individual a particular disambiguation model assigns to the name b, that object must also satisfy $\phi(x)$. So in that disambiguation model, $\phi(b)$ must be true. And since $\phi(b)$ lacked a truth value in the 'override' model M^R (since b is ambiguous), $\phi(b)$ is true in M^d-w.r.t.-M^R.

Case 2. Now consider the other case in which $\forall x \phi(x)$ is true in M^d-w.r.t.-M^R: $\forall x \phi(x)$ contains ambiguous words, and thus is not assigned a truth-value in M^R, but instead is only assigned the value *true* in the disambiguation model M^d. Now, every disambiguation model in isolation is a classical model, so if $\forall x \phi(x)$ is true in a particular M^d, then $\phi(b)$ must be true in that same M^d as well. But truth in M^d is not the same as M^d-w.r.t.-M^R, since truth-values in M^R override truth-values in M^d. However, given our assumptions, $\phi(b)$ must be truth-valueless in M^R, since if $\forall x \phi(x)$ contains ambiguous words, then $\phi(b)$ must contain ambiguous words as well. And if $\phi(b)$ contains ambiguous words, then it is truth-valueless in M^R (this step would be blocked if the language contained '=': 'Ant A = Charley' is false in M^R). Thus, since $\phi(b)$ is assigned no truth-value in M^R, but is true in M^d, $\phi(b)$ is true in M^d-w.r.t.-M^R in this second case as well.

Therefore, since these are the only two cases, the classical rule of $\forall$-elimination is sound on the semi-classical notion of logical consequence, and thus on the supervaluational notion of consequence as well. An analogous argument could be run for classical $\exists$-introduction, but I will not present it here, since it does not require any substantially different ideas.

References

Agar, N. (1993). What do frogs really believe? *Australasian Journal of Philosophy, 71*, 1–12.

Antonelli, A. (2000). Proto-semantics for positive free logic. *Journal of Philosophical Logic, 29*(3), 277–294.

Antonelli, A. (2007). Free quantification and logical invariance. *Rivista di Estetica, 34*, 61–73. doi.org/10.4000/estetica.3855.

Arenhart, J., & Arroyo, R. (Eds.). (2023). *Non-reflexive logics, non-individuals, and the philosophy of quantum mechanics*. Cham: Springer.

Bacon, A. (2013). Quantificational logic and empty names. *Philosophers' Imprint, 13*(24), 1–21.

Barker-Plummer, D., Barwise, J., & Etchemendy, J. (2011). *Language, proof, and logic* (Second ed.). Stanford, CA: CSLI Publications.

Beall, J. C. (2018). The simple argument for subclassical logic. *Philosophical Issues, 28*, 30–54.

Beall, J. C., & Restall, G. (2006). *Logical pluralism*. New York: Oxford University Press.

Bencivenga, E. (1981). Free semantics. In M. L. Dalla Chiara (Ed.), *Italian studies in the philosophy of science* (Vol. 47, pp. 31–48). Dordrecht: Reidel.

Bencivenga, E. (1990). Free from what? *Erkenntnis, 33*(1), 9–21.

Bencivenga, E. (2002). Free logics. In D. M. Gabbay & F. Guenthner (Eds.), *Handbook of philosophical logic* (Second ed., pp. 147–196). Dordrecht: Kluwer.

Bergman, K. (2023). Should the teleosemanticist be afraid of semantic indeterminacy? *Mind and Language, 38*, 296–314.

Berto, F. (2013). *Existence as a real property*. Dordrecht: Springer.

Boghossian, P. (1992). Externalism and inference. *Philosophical Issues, 2*, 11–28.

Bromwich, J. E., & Marcus, E. (2020). The anonymous professor who wasn't. *The New York Times*, August 4. www.nytimes.com/2020/08/04/style/college-coronavirus-hoax.html.

Braun, D. (1993). Empty names. *Noûs, 27*, 449–469.

Burge, T. (1974). Truth and singular terms. *Noûs, 8*, 309–325.

Burge, T. (1988). Individualism and self-knowledge. *Journal of Philosophy, 85*, 649–665.

Camp, J. (2002). *Confusion: A study in the theory of knowledge*. Cambridge, MA: Harvard University Press.

Carnap, R. (1956). *Meaning and necessity* (Second ed.). Chicago, IL: University of Chicago Press.

Chakrabarti, A. (1997). *Denying existence: The logic, epistemology and pragmatics of negative existentials and fictional discourse.* Dordrecht: Kluwer.

CIA (2016). Soviet jokes for the DDCI. CIA Freedom of Information Act Electronic Reading Room. December 27. www.cia.gov/readingroom/document/cia-rdp89g00720r000800040003-6.

Chang, H. (2003). Preservative realism and its discontents: Revisiting caloric. *Philosophy of Science, 70,* 902–912.

Clapp, L., Reimer, M., & Spire, A. (2019). Negative existentials. In J. Gundel & B. Abbott (Eds.), *The Oxford handbook of reference* (pp. 203–235). New York: Oxford University Press.

Coliva, A., & Belleri, D. (2013). Some observations on François Recanati's Mental Files. *Disputatio, V,* 103–113.

Dumitru, M., & Kroon, F. (2008). What to say when there is nothing to talk about. *Crítica: Revista Hispanoamericana de Filosofía, 40,* 97–109.

Dunn, J. M. (2000). Partiality and its dual. *Studia Logica, 66*(1), 5–40.

Dunn, J. M. (2021). R-Mingle is nice, and so is Arnon Avron. In O. Arieli & A. Zamansky (Eds.), *Arnon Avron on semantics and proof theory of non-classical logics* (pp. 141–165). Cham: Springer.

Dunn, J. M., & Restall, G. (2002). Relevance logic. In D. M. Gabbay & F. Guenthner (Eds.), *Handbook of philosophical logic* (Second ed., Vol. 6, pp. 1–128). Dordrecht: Kluwer.

Feyerabend, P. (1981). *Realism, rationalism and scientific method: Philosophical papers, vol. I.* Cambridge: Cambridge University Press.

Field, H. (1973). Theory change and indeterminacy of reference. *Journal of Philosophy, 70*(4), 462–481.

Fitting, M., & Mendelsohn, R. (1998). *First-order modal logic.* Dordrecht: Kluwer.

Frost-Arnold, G. (2014). Can the pessimistic induction be saved from semantic anti-realism about scientific theory? *British Journal for the Philosophy of Science, 65,* 521–548.

Frost-Arnold, G., & Beebe, J. (2020). Confused terms in ordinary language. *Journal of Logic, Language, and Information, 29,* 197–219.

Gilbert, D. (2020). QAnon's mysterious leader 'Q' is actually multiple people. Vice, December 16. www.vice.com/en/article/jgqj7x/qanons-mysterious-leader-q-is-actually-multiple-people.

Gómez-Torrente, M. (2019). Logical Truth. In E. N. Zalta (Ed.), *The Stanford encyclopedia of philosophy* (Spring 2019 ed.). Metaphysics

Research Lab, Stanford University, CA. https://plato.stanford.edu/archives/spr2019/entries/logical-truth/.

Gratzl, N. (2010). Sequent calculus for negative free logic. *Studia Logica, 96*, 331–348.

Hardegree, G. (2016). *Introduction to modal logic*. https://courses.umass.edu/phil511-gmh/text.htm.

Hazen, A. P., & Pelletier, F. J. (2014). Gentzen and Jaśkowski natural deduction: Fundamentally similar but importantly different. *Studia Logica, 102*(6), 1103–1142.

Hazen, A. P., & Pelletier, F. J. (2019). K3, Ł3, LP, RM3, A3, FDE, M: How to make many-valued logics work for you. In H. Omori & H. Wansing (Eds.), *New essays on Belnap-Dunn logic*. Cham: Springer.

Horn, L. (1989). *A natural history of negation*. Stanford, CA: CSLI Publications.

Indrzejczak, A., & Zawidzki, M. (2021). Tableaux for free logics with descriptions. In A. Das & S. Negri (Eds.), *Automated reasoning with analytic tableaux and related methods* (pp. 56–73). Cham: Springer.

Jeshion, R. (2015). Names not predicates. In A. Bianchi (Ed.), *On reference* (pp. 225–250). New York: Oxford University Press.

Kripke, S. (1977). Speaker's reference and semantic reference. *Midwest Studies in Philosophy, II*, 255–276.

Kaplan, D. (1990). Words. *Proceedings of the Aristotelian Society, 64*, 93–119.

Kroon, F. (1991). Denotation and description in free logic. *Theoria, 57*, 17–41.

Kuhn, T. (1977). Objectivity, value judgment, and theory choice. In *The essential tension* (pp. 320–339). Chicago, IL: University of Chicago Press.

Kürbis, N. (2021). Definite descriptions in intuitionist positive free logic. *Logic and Logical Philosophy, 30*, 327–358.

Lambert, K. (1972). Notes on free description theory: Some philosophical issues and consequences. *Journal of Philosophical Logic, 1*(2), 184–191. DOI 10.1007/bf00650497.

Lambert, K. (2001). Free logics. In L. Goble (Ed.), *The Blackwell guide to philosophical logic* (pp. 258–279). Malden, MA: Blackwell.

Lambert, K. (2002). Foundations of the hierarchy of free description theories. In *Free logic: Selected essays* (pp. 69–91). Cambridge: Cambridge University Press.

Lambert, K., & van Fraassen, B. C. (1972). *Derivation and counterexample: An introduction to philosophical logic*. Encino, CA: Dickenson Publishing Company.

Lawlor, K. (2007). A notional worlds approach to confusion. *Mind and Language, 22*(2), 150–172.

Lehmann, S. (1994). Strict Fregean free logic. *Journal of Philosophical Logic*, *23*, 307–336.

Lehmann, S. (2002). More free logic. In D. M. Gabbay & F. Guenthner (Eds.), *Handbook of philosophical logic* (Second ed., pp. 197–259). Dordrecht: Kluwer.

Lewis, D. K. (1982). Logic for equivocators. *Noûs*, *16*, 431–441.

Łukasiewicz, J. (1970). On three-valued logic. In L. Borkowski (Ed.), *Selected works*. Amsterdam: North-Holland Publishing.

MacFarlane, J. (2021). *Philosophical logic: A contemporary introduction*. New York: Routledge.

Maddy, P. (2007). *Second philosophy*. New York: Oxford University Press.

Magnus, P. D., Button, T., Loftis, J. R., Trueman, R., Thomas-Bolduc, A., & Zach, R. (2021). *Forallx: Calgary*. https://forallx.openlogicproject.org/forallxyyc.pdf.

Mares, E. (2020). Relevance logic. In E. N. Zalta (Ed.), *The Stanford encyclopedia of philosophy* (Winter 2020 ed.). Metaphysics Research Lab, Stanford University. https://plato.stanford.edu/archives/win2020/entries/logic-relevance/.

McLeish, C. (2006). Realism bit by bit: Disjunctive partial reference. *Studies in History and Philosophy of Science: Part A*, *37*, 171–190.

Meyer, R., Bencivenga, E., & Lambert, K. (1982). The ineliminability of E! in free quantification theory without identity. *The Journal of Philosophical Logic*, *11*, 229–231.

Meyer, R., & Lambert, K. (1968). Universally free logic and standard quantification theory. *The Journal of Symbolic Logic*, *33*, 8–26.

Morscher, E., & Simons, P. (2001). Free logic: A fifty-year past and an open future. In A. Hieke & E. Morscher (Eds.), *New essays in free logic* (pp. 1–34). Dordrecht: Kluwer.

Neander, K. (2017). *A mark of the mental: A defence of informational teleosemantics*. Cambridge, MA: MIT Press.

Nolt, J. (2010). Free logic. *Stanford Encyclopedia of Philosophy*. http://plato.stanford.edu/entries/logic-free/.

OrphAnalytics (2020). Style analysis by machine learning reveals that two authors likely shared the writing of QAnon's messages at two different periods in time. OrphAnalytics, December 15. www.orphanalytics.com/en/news/whitepaper202012/OrphAnalyticsQAnon2020.pdf.

Orlando, E. (2008). Fictional names without fictional objects. *Crítica: Revista Hispanoamericana de Filosofía*, *40*, 111–127.

Paoletti, M. P. (2016). A sketch of (an actually serious) Meinongian presentism. *Metaphysica*, *17*(1), 1–18.

Parsons, T. (1980). *Nonexistent objects*. New Haven, CT: Yale University Press.

Pavlović, E., & Gratzl, N. (2021). A more unified approach to free logics. *Journal of Philsophical Logic, 50*, 117–148.

Peacock, K., & Tedder, A. (2016). Identity, haecceity, and the Godzilla problem. In G. Payette (Ed.), *'Shut up,' he explained: Essays in honour of Peter K. Schotch* (pp. 63–79). London: College Publishers.

Pelletier, F. J., & Linsky, B. (2009). Russell vs. Frege on definite descriptions as singular terms. In N. Griffin & D. Jacquette (Eds.), *Russell vs. Meinong: The legacy of "On Denoting"*. New York: Routledge.

Piccinini, G., & Scott, S. (2010). Recovering what is said with empty names. *Canadian Journal of Philosophy, 40*(2), 239–274.

Priest, G. (1995). Multiple denotation, ambiguity, and the strange case of the missing amoeba. *Logique et Analyse, 150–152*, 361–373.

Priest, G. (2009). Not to be. In R. L. Poidevin, P. Simons, A. McGonigal, & R. Cameron (Eds.), *The Routledge companion to metaphysics* (pp. 234–245) New York: Routledge.

Priest, G. (2016). *Towards non-being* (Second ed.). New York: Oxford University Press.

Priest, G., Tanaka, K., & Weber, Z. (2022). Paraconsistent logic. In E. N. Zalta (Ed.), *The Stanford encyclopedia of philosophy* (Spring 2022 ed.). Metaphysics Research Lab, Stanford University. https://plato.stanford.edu/archives/spr2022/entries/logic-paraconsistent/.

Quine, W. V. O. (1960). *Word and object*. Cambridge, MA: Harvard University Press.

Recanati, F. (2012). *Mental files*. New York: Oxford University Press.

Restall, G. (2006). *Logic*. New York: Routledge.

Restall, G. (2019). Generality and existence 1: Quantification and free logic. *The Review of Symbolic Logic, 12*(1), 1–29.

Richardson, S. (2022). Sex contextualism. *Philosophy, Theory, and Practice in Biology, 14*(2). doi.org/10.3998/ptpbio.2096.

Ripley, D. (2018). Blurring: an approach to conflation. *Notre Dame Journal of Formal Logic, 59*(2), 171–188.

Routley, R. (1980). *Exploring Meinong's jungle and beyond*. Canberra: Australian National University, RSSS.

Rowbottom, D. (2011). The instrumentalist's new clothes. *Philosophy of Science, 78*(5), 1200–1211.

Rowbottom, D. (2019). *The instrument of science: Scientific anti-realism revitalized*. New York: Routledge.

Rowbottom, D. (2022). Can meaningless statements be approximately true? On relaxing the semantic component of scientific realism. *Philosophy of Science*, 1–18.

Rumfitt, I. (2003). Contingent existents. *Philosophy*, *78*, 461–481.

Sainsbury, M. (2004). Referring descriptions. In M. Reimer & A. Bezuidenhout (Eds.), *Descriptions and beyond.* New York: Oxford University Press.

Sainsbury, M. (2005). *Reference without referents.* New York: Oxford University Press.

Sankey, H. (1993). Kuhn's changing concept of incommensurability. *British Journal for the Philosophy of Science*, *44*(4), 759–774.

Sawyer, S. (2020). Names as predicates. In S. Biggs & H. Geirsson (Eds.), *Routledge handbook of linguistic reference* (pp. 198–212). New York: Routledge.

Schock, R. (1968). *Logics without existence assumptions*. Stockholm: Almqvist and Wiksells.

Schroeter, L. (2007). The illusion of transparency. *Australasian Journal of Philosophy*, *85*, 597–618.

Schulte, P., & Neander, K. (2022). Teleological theories of mental content. In E. N. Zalta (Ed.), *The Stanford encyclopedia of philosophy* (Summer 2022 ed.). Metaphysics Research Lab, Stanford University. https://plato.stanford.edu/archives/sum2022/entries/content-teleological/.

Smith, N. J. J. (2016). Truthier than thou: Truth, supertruth, and probability of truth. *Noûs*, *50*(4), 740–758.

Spencer, J. (2013). Unnecessary existents. *Canadian Journal of Philosophy*, *43*, 766–775.

Sullivan, M. (2012). Problems for temporary existence in tense logic. *Philosophy Compass*, *7*(1), 43–57.

Tedder, A. (2015). Axioms for finite collapse models of arithmetic. *The Review of Symbolic Logic*, *8*(3), 529–539.

Textor, M. (2016). Vacuous names in early analytic philosophy: Frege, Russell, Moore. *Philosophy Compass*, *11*(6), 316–326. doi.org/10.1111/phc3.12322

Troelstra, A. S., & van Dalen, D. (1988). *Constructivism in mathematics* (Vol. I). Amsterdam: Elsevier.

Unnsteinsson, E. (2022). *Talking about: An intentionalist theory of reference.* New York: Oxford University Press.

van Fraassen, B. (1966a). The completeness of free logic. *Zeitschrift für mathematische Logik und Grundlagen der Mathematik*, *12*, 219–234.

van Fraassen, B. (1966b). Singular terms, truth-value gaps, and free logic. *The Journal of Philosophy*, *63*, 481–495.

van Fraassen, B. (1980). *The scientific image.* New York: Oxford University Press.

Varzi, A. (2007). Supervaluationism and its logics. *Mind, 116*(463), 633–676.

Vickers, P. (2013). *Understanding inconsistent science.* New York: Oxford University Press.

von Fintel, K. (2004). Would you believe it? The king of France is back! Presuppositions and truth-value intuitions. In M. Reimer & A. Bezuidenhout (Eds.), *Descriptions and beyond* (pp. 315–341). New York: Oxford University Press.

von Wright, G. H. (Ed.). (1974). *Ludwig Wittgenstein: Letters to Russell, Keynes and Moore* (B. McGuinness, Trans.). Cornell, NY: Cornell University Press.

Williamson, T. (2002). Necessary existents. In A. O'Hear (Ed.), *Logic, thought, and language* (pp. 233–251). Cambridge: Cambridge University Press.

Williamson, T. (2013). *Modal logic as metaphysics.* New York: Oxford University Press.

Woodruff, P. (1984). On supervaluations in free logic. *Journal of Symbolic Logic, 49,* 943–950.

Wu, K. J. (1988). A basic free logic. *Notre Dame Journal of Formal Logic, 29*(4), 543–552.

Yablo, S. (2006). Non-catastrophic presupposition failure. In J. J. Thomson & A. Byrne (Eds.), *Content and modality: Themes from the philosophy of Robert Stalnaker.* New York: Oxford University Press.

Yi, B.-U. (2005). The logic and meaning of plurals. Part I. *Journal of Philosophical Logic, 34,* 459–506.

Zalta, E. (1983). *Abstract objects: An introduction to axiomatic metaphysics.* Dordrecht: Reidel.

Acknowledgments

Joseph Camp first helped me understand and appreciate the fascinating and difficult philosophical questions around confusion and ambiguity. Nuel Belnap was the first person to tell me, to my great surprise, that my ideas about the logic of non-univocal language might be publishable, and he helped me convert my inchoate, muddled ideas on this topic into something professional. Krista Lawlor provided extremely helpful input at an early stage of development. The participants of the Understanding Defectiveness in the Sciences Workshop, which took place at UNAM in 2019, helped me with the proof theory section. When thinking through the idea that classical logic gets the intuitive logical truths wrong (Section 2.2), Daniel Lindquist provided very useful and thoughtful defenses of the classical logician's point of view. Erin Kluge and Tayla Rossi went through the whole manuscript with a fine-toothed comb when it was near completion, and found several useful ways to improve it. I must thank Brad Armour-Garb and Fred Kroon, not only for the invitation to write this Element, but also for their patience, and their very valuable feedback at several stages of the writing process: They prevented this project from going off the rails more than once. The anonymous reviewers for this book improved it substantially; one reviewer in particular put in a great deal of time to correct several important oversights and mistakes in an earlier version. I am very grateful for their helpful and detailed criticisms. Finally, Karen Frost-Arnold was a very careful and insightful reader of the whole manuscript, consistently striking the right balance between reading sympathetically and reading critically. Her work created a much better finished product.

Cambridge Elements ⹀

Philosophy and Logic

Bradley Armour-Garb
SUNY Albany

Bradley Armour-Garb is chair and Professor of Philosophy at SUNY Albany. His books include *The Law of Non-Contradiction* (co-edited with Graham Priest and J. C. Beall, 2004), *Deflationary Truth* and *Deflationism and Paradox* (both co-edited with J. C. Beall, 2005), *Pretense and Pathology* (with James Woodbridge, Cambridge University Press, 2015), *Reflections on the Liar* (2017), and *Fictionalism in Philosophy* (co-edited with Fred Kroon, 2020).

Frederick Kroon
The University of Auckland

Frederick Kroon is Emeritus Professor of Philosophy at the University of Auckland. He has authored numerous papers in formal and philosophical logic, ethics, philosophy of language, and metaphysics, and is the author of *A Critical Introduction to Fictionalism* (with Stuart Brock and Jonathan McKeown-Green, 2018).

About the Series

This Cambridge Elements series provides an extensive overview of the many and varied connections between philosophy and logic. Distinguished authors provide an up-to-date summary of the results of current research in their fields and give their own take on what they believe are the most significant debates influencing research, drawing original conclusions.

Cambridge Elements ≡

Philosophy and Logic

Printed in the United States
by Baker & Taylor Publisher Services